DISCOVER
DEVON
FROM ABOVE

Contents

MYRIAD

LONDON

North Devon

The birthplace of a saint, the UK's oldest borough, the country's best beach and the starting point for one of the toughest challenges for youngsters are all to be found in north Devon. The north Devon coastline is one of the most rugged and dramatic in England; it is also the highest. Tucked away along the coast are sheltered coves offering a safe haven for shipping, while the west-facing sandy beaches are the favourite haunts of swimmers and surfers. The wilds of Exmoor contrast with the more gentle countryside along the meandering valleys of the rivers Taw and Torridge. Historic towns and picturesque villages complete the picture and are the reason that visitors return year after year.

Foreland Point The rocky headland of Foreland Point (left) two miles east off Lynmouth is the most northerly point on the Devon coast. It is also the most northerly point of the Exmoor National Park and separates Lynmouth Bay from Countisbury Cove. The highest cliff rises 292ft (89m) above the high water line, but the highest point of the whole headland, at 991ft (302m), is further inland near the tiny village of Countisbury. The Exmoor Heritage Coast extends to the east and west of Foreland Point and is England's highest coastline. Located 220ft (67m) above the high tide but well below the crest of the headland sits the Lynmouth Foreland lighthouse. Established in 1900, the lighthouse was automated in 1994 and is now controlled by the Trinity House Operations Control Centre in Essex. The headland gives wonderful views across Lynmouth Bay and the coast of South Wales is usually clearly visible to the north.

Lynton and Lynmouth The pretty harbour village of Lynmouth (above) sits at the confluence of the East and West Lynn rivers and is sheltered by Foreland Point. The wooded hillsides, narrow valleys and gushing rivers led the Victorians to call this part of the coast "little Switzerland". Thomas Gainsborough spent his honeymoon in Lynmouth and described it as "the most beautiful place for a landscape painter this country can boast". Disaster struck Lynmouth on 15 and 16 August 1952. After nine inches of rain, a raging torrent raced through the village, causing heavy damage and the loss of 34 lives. The village was rebuilt after the flooding and the river diverted around the village. Five hundred feet (152m) above Lynmouth is its sister village of Lynton (left and top), a popular holiday destination in Victorian times. In order to ease visitors' journeys up the cliff from the harbour an ingenious cliff railway was opened in 1890.

Combe Martin and Ilfracombe Set on the
western edge of Exmoor, Combe Martin (above) boasts the
longest main road of any village in England. It runs through
the village along the valley of the river Umber for over two
miles (3km). Taking pride of place are the 13th century
St Peter ad Vincular church and the 17th century Pack
o'Cards Inn, which was built by George Ley of Marwood
in celebration of a large win at cards. Today at the Combe
Martin Wildlife & Dinosaur Park visitors can see the
country's first animatronic Tyrannosaurus Rex. Further
west along the coast lies Ilfracombe (right), which featured
as *Alfreinscoma* in the Exeter Domesday Book of 1086.
This colourful holiday resort with its floral displays has
frequently won the Britain in Bloom competition. Its
harbour, the largest on the north Devon coast, is protected
from the east by Hillsborough Hill which is 447ft (136m)
high. Ilfracombe's oldest building, St Nicholas' Chapel, sits
on the smaller Lantern Hill, which protects the harbour
from the Bristol Channel. The architecturally striking
Landmark Theatre overlooking the seafront opened in
1998 and is still a source of controversy. Between March
and October you can take the ferry between Ilfracombe
and Lundy Island.

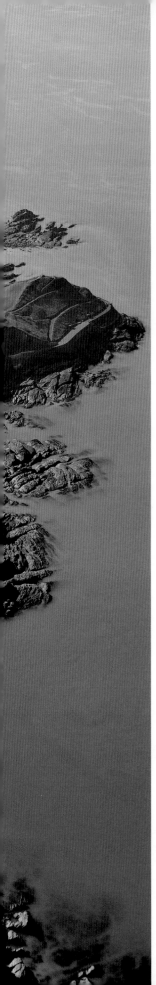

Woolacombe Village Beach and Barnstaple The sandy beach at Woolacombe (above) extends two and a quarter miles (3.5km) along Morte Bay between Baggy and Morte Points. This Blue Flag beach has long been a favourite with surfers and has been voted one of the best beaches in the country. During the Second World War Woolacombe was home to the US Army Training Centre. Troops practised here for the D-Day landings as the long beach closely resembled the landing area at Omaha Beach in Normandy.

Barnstaple (below), on the banks of the river Taw, claims to be the UK's oldest borough. It has been the major market in the area since Saxon times, and the Domesday Book records that it had a mint. By the Middle Ages Barnstaple had become an important trading centre for wool. The town's status as a market centre was further enhanced in 1855 with the building of Butcher's Row and Pannier Market. Today some of the 33 shops in Butchers Row still trade as butchers, while others sell local produce. The Pannier Market is still held three times a week and it has been rated as one of the best food markets in the country. Traffic congestion in Barnstaple was finally eased in May 2007 with the opening of the western bypass. The five spans of the quarter-mile long (409m) Downstream Bridge carry traffic over the river Taw away from the town centre.

Tiverton Tiverton's roots go back to the Stone Age. Its name is derived from *Twyverton*, meaning the town on two fords – in this case on the rivers Lowman and Exe. Tiverton Castle was built on the orders of Henry I in 1106 and in the Middle Ages it was home to the powerful Earls of Devon. In the 16th and 17th centuries Tiverton prospered due to the wool trade, but declined during the Industrial Revolution. By the 1850s Tiverton was on the way up again, with a new lace industry and the arrival of a branch of the Great Western Canal (above centre). From 1835-1865 Lord Palmerston was the MP for Tiverton. Renowned for his interventionist "gunboat diplomacy", Palmerston served as Foreign Secretary for some 20 years followed by two periods as Prime Minister when Queen Victoria's empire was at its peak. Tiverton kept its own independent police force until 1945.

Okehampton Like many towns in the region, Okehampton's early prosperity was based on the wool trade. On the northern edge of Dartmoor, the town lies on the river Okement, from where it gets its name. Okehampton Castle was the only castle to be listed in the Domesday Book. Its keep was extended by the 1st Earl of Devon, Sir Robert de Courtenay, in the 14th century but only ruins remain. Today Okehampton (below) is known for its broad main street, Fore Street (bottom), and its Victorian shopping arcade. Outside the town, Okehampton camp on Dartmoor is a major army-training base. Each May hundreds of youngsters set off from here on the Ten Tors Challenge.

Crediton Lying in the vale of the river Creedy, Crediton (left) is known as the birthplace of St Boniface, the patron saint of Germany and Holland, in about 672. The Diocese of Crediton was created in 909 with Edwulf as the first bishop here to cover Devon and Cornwall. The seat was transferred to Exeter in 1050. The cathedral may have occupied the site of what is now Crediton parish church formally known as "the Church of the Holy Cross and the Mother of Him who hung thereon". Today the suffragan Bishop of Crediton assists the diocesan Bishop of Exeter. The pioneering engineer Isambard Kingdom Brunel designed Crediton's station, which is served by two railway lines. The Tarka Line from Exeter through Crediton to Barnstaple follows the rivers Yeo and Taw. The Dartmoor Railway, a heritage line, runs services to Okehampton and is now owned by British American Railway Services.

Lundy Island This mainly granite island, rich in fauna and flora, is 12 miles (19km) off the coast, about one third of the way across the Bristol Channel between Pembrokeshire and north Devon. The name Lundy may come from the Norse for puffin, and there is a small colony of puffins on the island today. The island has a very chequered history: times of turmoil when it was run by pirates and privateers contrasted with times of peace when it was owned by private families. In the late 19th century Lundy's rector was Thomas Heaven, and some people referred to the island as the Kingdom of Heaven. Today the National Trust owns Lundy Island, and just 28 people live there. The Landmark Trust manages 23 holiday properties on the island and owns the main means of transport to the mainland, the MS *Oldenburg*. Most of the accommodation is located in the south of the island and ranges from a 13th century castle to an old lighthouse and a Georgian-style villa. Lundy features as a sea area in the UK shipping forecast. Two lighthouses warn shipping of the island's 20 miles (32km) of dangerous coastline: Lundy North and Lundy South, which both date from 1897.

Above left: the majestic glory of Lundy Island.
Above: St Helena's church and the Georgian-style Millcombe House surrounded by trees.
Far left: Lundy North lighthouse with the Hen and Chickens rocks in the foreground.
Left: Jenny's Cove with Pyramid rock on Lundy's west coast.
Right: Beacon Hill, the highest point on the island.

Plymouth & Dartmoor

The Dartmoor National Park dominates South Devon. Covering 368 square miles, the park mainly consists of wild peaty moorland covering an underlying granite landmass. Occasionally, the granite protrudes through the surface, particularly at the highest points of the moor, giving rise to the rounded rocky tors which are such a distinctive feature of Dartmoor. To the south-west of this rugged and challenging countryside, close to the border with Cornwall, lies Plymouth, the largest city of the south-west. The city has played a central part in Britain's naval history and Devonport is the largest naval base in Western Europe.

Naval Dockyard The four miles (6km) of waterfront, five basins, 14 dry docks and 25 tidal berths of the Royal Naval Dockyard (above and bottom right) cover 650 acres. Her Majesty's Naval Base Devonport is the largest in Western Europe. The Devonport flotilla includes 11 frigates, seven Trafalgar class nuclear submarines and the navy's largest ship, HMS *Ocean*. Every two years the public can visit the dockyards on Navy Day, the Royal Navy's biggest public event. Devonport and Stonehouse are the settlements that grew into the present-day city of Plymouth. Originally a fishing village, Stonehouse started to develop with the completion of three military facilities: the Royal Naval Hospital in 1762, the Royal Marine barracks in 1783 and the Royal William Victualling Yard in 1835. The naval dockyards were established on the orders of King William III in 1691. The original name of Plymouth Dock was changed to Devonport in 1823 at the request of local residents. Of the three, only the barracks are still in use today. The 16-acre Royal William Victualling Yard served as stores for food, drink and munitions for the navy. It closed in 1992, and is now undergoing a £110m regeneration including residential and office space. Close by, ferries leave from Millbay docks bound for Roscoff in France and Santander in Spain.

Tamar Bridge From shortly after its source at East Youlstone, four miles (6km) from the north Cornish coast, the river Tamar forms most of the border between the counties of Cornwall and Devon. The most spectacular of the 20 road bridges over the river is the Tamar Bridge (left). When it opened in 1961, its central span of 1100 feet (335m) made it the UK's longest suspension bridge. Vehicles pay a toll only when leaving Cornwall. Before the bridge opened, motorists who wanted to travel between Plymouth and Saltash (on the Cornish side of the Tamar) had to endure a long drive north or use the car ferry across the river. To the seaward side of the road bridge, Isambard Kingdom Brunel's Royal Albert Bridge carries the Cornish main railway line from Saltash over to Plymouth. The rail bridge was opened by Prince Albert in 1859, the year of Brunel's death.

Plymouth Strategically important for centuries, Plymouth is situated between the rivers Tamar and Plym, where they flow into Plymouth Sound, the massive bay which provides a natural deep-water harbour, ideal for large naval craft. Plymouth was mentioned in the Domesday Book and in 1439 was the first town in the country to receive its charter; it became a city in 1928. The Royal Citadel (below) on the waterfront was built in 1665 by Charles II in anticipation of a Dutch invasion. The 70ft (21m) high walls made it the country's most important fortification for over 100 years. During the 1750s, 113 guns were added. The citadel is still used today, and is open to visitors during the summer. The adjacent green space is Plymouth Hoe. Here, in 1588, Sir Francis Drake is said to have insisted on completing his game of bowls before he set sail to confront the Spanish Armada. Today you will find Drake's statue, together with the red and white Smeaton's tower, which used to guard the Eddystone Rocks nine miles (14km) offshore. Projecting out into Plymouth Sound is the almost circular 1930s art deco Tinside Pool. This stunning lido re-opened to the public in 2005 after a £3.4m renovation.

The Barbican

The area to the north and west of the former harbour of Plymouth is known as the Barbican and is steeped in history. For centuries this was home to Plymouth's fishermen and fish market. To the left of the entry lock to what is now the 467-berth Sutton Harbour Marina (pictured above) are the Mayflower Steps. The Pilgrim Fathers sailed from here in *The Mayflower* in 1620 to establish the new colony of Plymouth in modern-day Massachusetts. Also in the Barbican is the Black Friars distillery where Plymouth gin has been made since 1793. Due to its naval importance, Plymouth was heavily bombed by the Germans during the Second World War. The first bombs fell on the city on 6 July 1940 and the last of the 59 raids that became known as the Plymouth Blitz came on 30 April 1944. Much of the city centre was reduced to rubble, 1,172 civilians were killed and 4,448 injured. After the war the city centre (above left) was rebuilt according to plans drawn up by Sir Patrick Abercrombie. As a reminder of the devastation caused by the war, the ruins of Charles Church stand guard on one of the city's roundabouts (right). Consecrated in 1665 and the second oldest parish church in Plymouth, it was almost destroyed by bombs during the nights of 21 and 22 March 1941. A recent addition to the Plymouth skyline is the National Marine Aquarium across from the Mayflower Steps. Britain's largest aquarium, it opened in 1998.

Tavistock The market town of Tavistock (above), on the western edge of Dartmoor on the river Tavy, traces its roots back to the founding of an abbey, now ruined, in AD961. In the 14th century Tavistock was a mining town, one of Europe's largest sources of tin where the metal was weighed and stamped. Tavistock's most illustrious son, Sir Francis Drake, was born at Crowndale Farm around 1540. Drake was to become the first Englishman to circumnavigate the world, a journey which lasted from 1577 until 1580. The viaduct seen in the left of the picture once carried trains on the Plymouth Devonport and South Western Junction Railway; it opened in 1890. Today it is part of the national cycle network's route 27. At the annual Tavistock food festival growers from Cornwall, Devon, Dorset and Somerset promote and sell their quality produce.

King's Tor One of the many of Dartmoor's famous tors, the 1314ft (400m) high King's Tor (below) lies to the south-east of Merrivale. It is encircled by the Dartmoor Way foot and cycle path.

Dartmeet The woody setting of Dartmeet (right) in the heart of Dartmoor is well named: it is the meeting point of the East and West Dart rivers. From here the river Dart flows down off the moor southeastwards through Buckfastleigh and Totnes before reaching the sea beyond Dartmouth. Beside an ancient, partially collapsed clapper bridge, a more substantial twin-arched bridge carries the road over the East Dart. Dartmeet, which is a popular spot for visitors, forms the northern gateway to the Dart Valley Nature Reserve. Upstream is the Badger's Holt tea room, said to be "the most famous tea room on Dartmoor", which offers Devon cream teas prepared to a secret 50-year-old recipe.

Dartmoor Prison High up on the moor, Dartmoor Prison (above) dominates the village of Princetown. One of Britain's most famous prisons, Dartmoor's reputation has been enhanced by its remote location. It was built between 1806 and 1809. The first occupants were French and American prisoners of war, from the Napoleonic Wars and the War of 1812 respectively. Owned by the Duchy of Cornwall, the prison is now a category C establishment. In the annual Dartmoor Jailbreak, a charity event, teams of two or more people – not inmates – in prison uniform compete for the furthest distance travelled without paying for their transport. The record so far is New Zealand!

Dartmoor Created in 1951, Dartmoor National Park is one of the country's last remaining wildernesses. It covers an area of 368 square miles and is rich in wildlife and archaeological remains. The highest point on the moor is at High Willhays, 2040ft (621m) above sea level. More than half of the national park is private land, owned by such bodies as the Duchy of Cornwall and the Ministry of Defence. Since 1985 walkers have been free to roam where they wish and the moor's 450 miles (720km) of bridleways and paths are for guidance only. Over 29,000 people live within Dartmoor, which is also home to the native Dartmoor pony. These ponies are all owned by local farmers, who mark them either by tagging or cutting their tail hair in a distinctive way. A particular feature of Dartmoor are its exposed and windswept tors, large hills usually topped with rocky outcrops. There are over 160 tors, the best known of which is Hay Tor (above and left) at 1500ft (457m). Stone from the nearby granite quarries was used to build the first London Bridge in 1831. Close by is Hound Tor (below left), another fine example of a Dartmoor Tor. At the beginning of May, thousands of 14- to 20-year-olds, in teams of six, gather at the army base at Okehampton to embark on the annual Ten Tors Challenge. In the course of 24 hours they must visit 10 tors on a set route, carrying all their supplies and equipment with them. The arduous terrain, frequent high winds and driving rain make this quite a challenge.

Uncle Tom Cobley and all came to Widecombe Fair, according to the 1880 folk song. The annual agricultural fair at Widecombe-in-the-Moor (right) continues on the second Tuesday in September, with maypole dancing and bale tossing. The 120ft (37m) tower of St Pancras church, known as the Cathedral of the Moors, can be seen from afar.

Grimspound Just below Hameldown Tor in the north-west of
Dartmoor lie the late Bronze Age remains of Grimspound (above).
It is a massive granite wall surrounding 24 hut circles, thought to have
been settled around 1300BC. One hut still features a doorway with two
stone uprights. Reverend Richard Polwhele first named the settlement
Grimspound in his 1797 *History of Devon*. The name possibly derives
from Grim, the Anglo-Saxon god of war, more widely known as Odin.

Buckfast Abbey There has been an abbey at Buckfast (above) since
1018. The first monks were Benedictines: 343 years after the Dissolution
of the Monasteries in 1539 they returned in 1882. Today the abbey is
renowned for its honey and its colony of honeybees, and also for its
tonic wine – the development of which is attributed to French monks
who settled at the abbey in the 1880s.

The South Hams

This beautiful region sits on a broad peninsula at the southernmost tip of Devon. With its unspoilt beaches, clifftop scenery and fine towns, the South Hams area has a well-deserved reputation as one of the most idyllic parts of the south-west. There seems to be water seems at every turn in South Hams due to the indented coastline. Even the towns of Kingsbridge and Totnes are linked to the sea by the deep valleys of the Kingsbridge and Dart estuaries. The area also contains Britain's premier naval training college at Dartmouth plus the beautiful and atmospheric seaside port of Salcombe.

Burgh Island Just 656ft (200m) offshore from Bigbury-on-Sea sits Burgh Island (above). The island's buildings include the Pilchard Inn pub and the art deco Burgh Island Hotel, dating from 1929. At low tide visitors can walk to the island; at other times the hotel operates a sea-tractor service, seen above in mid-crossing. The first sea-tractor was built in 1930 and today's vehicle dates from 1969. The driver and passengers sit on an elevated platform, whilst the Fordson tractor powered wheelbase crosses the sand underwater. During the Second World War wounded RAF personnel would come to Burgh Island Hotel to convalesce. Agatha Christie visited the island and used it as the setting for two of her books.

Bantham and Thurlestone The sandy beaches at Bantham (above) and Thurlestone are some of the best on the South Devon coast and the Blue Flag Bantham beach has excellent surfing and windsurfing. The village of Bantham itself lies upstream from the coast, on the banks of the unspoilt river Avon. Thurlestone takes its name from an arch-shaped rock, or "thirled stone", just offshore in the bay (shown bottom left below). The village's two beaches are separated by the Thurlestone golf course; its third hole is played out on Warren Point.

Kingsbridge and the Kingsbridge Estuary The market town of Kingsbridge lies at the northern end of the Kingsbridge estuary, six miles (10km) from the sea. The estuary (below), noted for its creeks and side channels, is situated in the South Devon area of outstanding natural beauty. Kingsbridge derives its name from a 10th century bridge linking the royal estates of Alvington and Chillington. The Abbot of Buckfast was granted permission for a market here in 1219. The monks sold honey, cream and scones and this market tradition, including a farmers' market, continues every Tuesday and Saturday. The town centre (right) features several 18th and 19th century buildings including the Shambles market arcade. Running off Fore Street are intriguingly named passages such as Western Backway and Squeeze Belly Alley.

Salcombe Close to the mouth of the Kingsbridge estuary, Salcombe (above) has a proud tradition as a boatbuilding and seafaring port. Several ships lie wrecked in the surrounding waters including a Bronze Age ship, one of only three known in the country. By the 19th century Salcombe had become an important centre for the fruit trade and the local boatyards were busy producing the Salcombe schooner. These fast vessels brought oranges and lemons from the Azores and pineapples from the Bahamas. However the boatyards found themselves unable to compete with the iron and steel craft of the northern and Scottish shipyards, so they reverted to producing fishing and sailing boats, which they continue to do. Because of its popularity amongst the sailing fraternity, property prices in Salcombe are the second-highest outside central London, after those of Sandbanks in Dorset.

Start Bay Start Point (above) juts almost claw-like about a mile out into the sea at the southern end of Start Bay, which in turn extends northwards round the coast to the Dart estuary. It is one of the most exposed peninsulas in the country. To warn of the dangers to shipping, a lighthouse was built in 1836 high on the headland, almost at the cliff edge. Designed by James Walker, it features a notable battlemented parapet. Almost at the end of the cliffs in the picture above lies the deserted village of Hallsands. Little is known of the early history of the village; by 1891 it had 37 houses. In 1900 heavy storms washed away the sea wall and 16 years later further gales and high tides broke through the village's sea defences, leaving only one property habitable. To the north of the rocks of Tinsey Head sits the fishing village of Beesands (right), known today for its lobster and crab fishing.

Torcross Continuing around Start Bay, you reach the village of Torcross (above and inset), on the shores of the south-west's largest freshwater lake, Slapton Ley. Only the shingle beach of Slapton Sands separates this national nature reserve from the sea. In 1943 Torcross was used by 15,000 allied troops as a practice ground for the Normandy landings. But tragedy struck on 28 April 1944 when German submarines intercepted a convoy of ships taking part in these D-Day rehearsals, sinking two tank landing ships with the loss of 749 American lives. At the northern end of the bay lies the inviting beach of Blackpool Sands (right).

Dartmouth and Kingswear

The town of Dartmouth (right) lies on the west bank of the Dart estuary. The narrow Dart estuary is guarded by two castles. Set on a rocky promontory, Dartmouth castle started life in 1388 as a coastal fort. Henry VIII added gun platforms during the 16th century. The tower of the adjacent St Petroc's church overlooks the castle. Naval officer training in Dartmouth goes back to 1863 when two vessels were moored on the river. The Royal Naval College (left), designed by Sir Aston Webb, was built in 1905 and overlooks the town. On the opposite bank of the Dart estuary lies Kingswear, connected to Dartmouth by three ferries. The village was the final stop on the Dartmouth & Torbay Railway, which opened in 1864. The line faced closure in 1968 and was purchased in 1972 by the Dart Valley Railway Company. It is now the Paignton & Dartmouth Steam Railway, and is a great tourist attraction. Due to local opposition the station at Dartmouth never saw a train and the pretty building is today a café.

Totnes Located at the highest navigable point and the lowest bridging point at the head of the Dart estuary, Totnes can trace its roots back to 907 when its first castle was built by the Breton, Juhel of Totnes. By the 12th century Totnes was an important market town and remains so today. Regular markets are held every Friday and Saturday in the town's square, bordered by the Civic Hall. The town's many impressive buildings include a number of Elizabethan merchant's houses and the Eastgate, which spans the High Street. Totnes is on the main London to Penzance railway line, but it was also on the Buckfastleigh, Totnes & South Devon Railway which opened in 1872. A casualty of the Beeching cuts in the 1960s, the line reopened as the Dart Valley Railway in 1969 with steam trains once again running between Totnes and Buckfastleigh. Renamed the South Devon Railway, the line was acclaimed Heritage Railway of the Year 2007.

South Devon

Stretching from Berry Head to Seaton, close to the border with Dorset, this area centres on the city of Exeter. It boasts an outstanding coastline which can be divided into two parts – the English Riviera which stretches along Tor Bay with the resorts of Torquay, Paignton and Brixham and to the east the start of the Jurassic coast which includes Exmouth, Budleigh Salterton, Ladram Bay, Sidmouth, Branscombe, Beer and Seaton.

Berry Head This limestone peninsula (left) forms the southern extremity of Torbay and rises 200ft (65m) above the sea. Berry Head is a national nature reserve: its thin soil and mild climate encourage rare plants, and the surrounding cliffs boast colonies of guillemots, black-legged kittiwakes and razorbills. The headland is guarded by Napoleonic fortifications, built between 1795 and 1806. At the other end of the headland sits the Berry Head lighthouse, the smallest, highest and deepest lighthouse in the British Isles. It dates from 1906 and is just 16ft (5m) high, but sits 190ft (58m) above the mean high water line.

Torquay At the northern end of Tor Bay, Torquay (right and below) boasts over 500 hotels and more Blue Flag beaches than any other British seaside resort. The distinctive cabbage trees (*cordyline australis*) which give the town a Mediterranean feel, were introduced from New Zealand in 1820 and have thrived in the mild climate and long hours of sunshine. The town started its life as a holiday resort in the 19th century. The first visitors were the families of naval officers whose ships were anchored in the bay during the Napoleonic wars. In the First World War survivors of the Battle of Gallipoli recuperated in military hospitals, and during the Second World War evacuees arrived from London. Over 23,000 US troops left Torquay for Utah Beach in Normandy in the D-Day landings in 1944. Four years later, Torquay staged the aquatic events of the London Olympics. Torquay is the birthplace of the novelist Agatha Christie and the writer and comedian Peter Cook.

Brixham The busy fishing port and town of Brixham (above) lies at the southern end of Torbay. It featured as *Briseham* in the Domesday Book, with a population of just 39. In the town centre today stands a statue of William of Orange, later William III of England, who landed here on November 5 1688 with an army of 20,000 men and 5,000 horses. Many locals have Dutch surnames, a sign that they are descendants of soldiers in his army. Brixham is said to be the "mother of deep-sea fisheries" as its boats helped develop such ports as Hull and Grimsby and today it has a small fleet of vintage restored vessels.

Dawlish Warren The sandy spit that is Dawlish Warren (below right) stretches for two miles (3km) out into the mouth of the Exe estuary. The long sandy beach is popular with families and is backed by an 18-hole golf course and a nature reserve. The 500-acre reserve boasts over 450 different plant species, including the unique Warren crocus, which is protected by Act of Parliament. The neighbouring dunes are home to large numbers of birds, both indigenous and migratory. The railway line from Exeter to Paignton is promoted as the Riviera Line. It follows the Exe estuary and then cuts behind Langstone Rock (left) before hugging the coast beyond Dawlish Warren to Teignmouth.

Exeter The county town of Devon, Exeter's roots are probably Celtic in origin. The Celts gave way to the Romans, who founded their city of *Isca Dumnoniorum* on the banks of the Exe in AD50. The city was at the southern end of the Fosse Way Roman road and parts of the Roman walls can still be seen today. Pride of place in the city centre goes to Exeter's Anglican cathedral, dedicated to St Peter (shown centre above). It was founded in 1050 when the episcopal seat was moved from Crediton to Exeter. The first Bishop of Exeter, Leofric, was personally installed by Edward the Confessor. The building we see today dates from 1400 and boasts the longest vaulted ceiling in the country. Early in Exeter's history, the tidal river Exe was navigable right up to the city walls and it was a busy port. But over the centuries weirs were built in the river to control its flow, and trade was threatened. This was resolved by building the canal, completed in 1567 and featuring the country's first pound locks. Miller's Crossing bridge, a new pedestrian and cycle bridge (shown bottom right), opened in 2002.

City Centre With the arrival of the railways in 1844, Exeter continued to thrive and grow as a trading centre. Today the city's two mainline stations, Exeter St David's and Exeter Central, link it not only to London and Plymouth but also to Bristol, Birmingham and the North. Exeter suffered 18 German bombing raids during the Second World War and much of the city centre was flattened. The cathedral also received a direct hit but has been fully restored. In the 1950s the area between the cathedral and the High Street was developed and became the Princesshay pedestrian shopping precinct, the first of its kind in the country. A £200m redevelopment in 2007 has resulted in Princesshay's revival as a more modern shopping centre (below). In addition to three major stores and 60 other shops, along with cafés and restaurants, the new development also includes 123 one- and two-bedroom apartments. In 2004 Exeter became a Fairtrade Town. Today Exeter's three largest employers are the university, Devon County Council and the Meteorological Office or Met Office, the UK's weather forecasting service, which moved from Bracknell in 2004.

Exmouth The attractive holiday resort of Exmouth is situated by the sea at the mouth of the river Exe. With its varied architecture and location the town became popular when the railway arrived in 1861. The marina was converted from the old docks in 2002. Orcombe Point in Exmouth is the starting point for the Jurassic Coast, a World Heritage Site stretching for 95 miles (153km) to the dramatic Old Harry Rocks in Dorset.

Budleigh Salterton The elderly residents of Budleigh Salterton (right) give the resort a genteel air. Red Devonian sandstone cliffs bookend the town's pebble beach which runs for 2.5 miles (4km) to the mouth of the river Otter at Otterhead. A short distance to the north of Budleigh is Hayes Barton, birthplace of Walter Raleigh. Sir John Everett Millais captured a moment in Raleigh's childhood in his painting *The Boyhood of Raleigh*, which hangs at Tate Britain in London.

Sidmouth Featuring in the Domesday Book as the fishing village of *Sedmuda*, Sidmouth (above) developed into a fashionable holiday resort in the 18th and 19th centuries. Today the fine Georgian and Regency villas on the promenade are hotels. At the western edge of the town, the pebble beach gives way to sand at Jacob's Ladder, which is accessed from the clifftop gardens by a steep wooden staircase. The town's folk festival, held every August, has grown in scope and reputation: from lowly beginnings in 1955 it has become the Sidmouth International Folklore Festival. To the east of the town rises the mighty Salcombe Hill Cliff (below). A red Devon sandstone cliff, it dates from the Triassic period and is characteristic of the cliffs on this section of the World Heritage Jurassic Coast. To the west, in Ladram Bay, there are several offshore stacks, such as Big Picket Rock which rises 140ft (43m).

Beer The unspoilt fishing village of Beer (above and right) was once surrounded by forests, and takes its name from the Anglo-Saxon word *bere* or *beare* meaning woodland. It is sheltered from the prevailing winds by Beer Head and the high cliffs nearby. The village thrived on fishing and smuggling. Jack Rattenbury, Devon's most notorious smuggler, was born in Beer in 1778 and visitors can still see the caves where contraband goods were stored. All fishing boats have to be hauled up on to the beach as there is no harbour. Twenty-four of Britain's cathedrals and famous buildings have used stone quarried in Beer; they include Exeter cathedral, St Paul's, the Tower of London and Windsor castle. Stone has been quarried here since Roman times. At Pecorama, above Beer, young and old can enjoy a ride on the Beer Heights light railway, which opened in 1975.

BROAD GAUGE LOCOMOTIVES

Geof Sheppard

Published by

NOODLE BOOKS

in conjunction with

© Geof Sheppard and Noodle Books 2008

ISBN   978-1-906419-09-7

First published in 2008 by Kevin Robertson
under the **NOODLE BOOKS** imprint
PO Box 279
Corhampton
SOUTHAMPTON
SO32 3ZX

www.kevinrobertsonbooks.co.uk

Printed in England by the Alden Press

Front cover - *Pearson 2-4-0, (B31), No 2018, formerly Bristol & Exeter Railway, No 6, on shed at Bristol.*
Original painting by Paul Garnsworthy.

Rear cover - *The Firefly and Iron Duke replicas have given us a chance to see and ride behind broad gauge locomotives, they also demonstrate how fast technology was changing in the 1840s. Firefly, in steam at Didcot Railway Centre, is closely copied from a Priam class 7ft 2-2-2 built in 1840 with a haycock firebox and an 8ft 6in x 4ft 0in boiler working at 50lbs per square inch. On display in the National Railway Museum in York is Iron Duke, based on an Alma class 8ft 4-2-2 built just seven years later with a round topped firebox and an 11ft x 4ft 9¾in 100lb boiler.*
Photographs by Alan Garner and Geof Sheppard

The Broad Gauge Society exists to promote the research and modelling of 7ft 0¼in gauge railways.

To find out more, visit our website at

www.broadgauge.org.uk

CONTENTS

BIBLIOGRAPHY

Ahrons, EL, *Locomotive and Train Working in the Latter Part of the Nineteenth Century, Volume 4* (Heffer 1953)

Chapman, WG, *Locos of the Royal Road* (GWR 1936)

Industrial Railway Society, *Industrial Locomotives of South Western England* (IRS 1977)

Lyons, E & Mountford, E, *Great Western Engine Sheds 1837-1947*, (OPC 1979, revised 1986))

MacDermot, ET, *History of the Great Western Railway* (two volumes; GWR 1927 & 1931)

Maggs, C, *The Bristol and Gloucester Railway* (Oakwood Press 1992)

Nicholas, J, *The North Devon Line* (OPC 1992)

Railway Correspondence & Travel Society, *The Locomotives of the Great Western Railway, Part 2 Broad Gauge* (RCTS 1952)

Railway Correspondence & Travel Society, *The Locomotives of the Great Western Railway, Part 3 Absorbed Engines 1854-1921* (RCTS 1956)

Sharman, M, *The Broad Gauge of the Great Western Railway, the Bristol & Exeter Railway and the North and South Devon Railways* (Oakwood Press 1985)

Waters, L, *The Great Western Broad Gauge* (Ian Allan 1999)

Various articles in *Broadsheet*, *Locomotive Magazine*, and *Railway Magazine*

The *Alma* class renewals *(A18)* were active right up to the last day of broad gauge operations, when *Dragon* posed at *Taunton*. It has been possible to see an 8ft single again since the construction of the 'Iron Duke replica (A91) for the GW150 celebrations in 1985.

When Isambard Kingdom Brunel ordered the first locomotives for his daring 7ft gauge railway, the technology to power express trains was in its infancy. By the end of the broad gauge era, a little over half a century later, locomotive design had matured so that most of the later locomotives do not look too different from many of those running in the first half of the twentieth century. Indeed some of them were still running then, having been converted to run on the 4ft 8½in standard gauge (or "narrow gauge" as it was called until 1892).

Through all this change the wide choice of locomotive names stayed constant. A pantheon of gods' names was mixed with famous people, places (not always served by the railway), flora and fauna. To confuse matters more, names would be passed from one locomotive to another to help accountants monitor capital costs, and different railways would use the same names.

This book tries to bring together for the first time information about all the 7ft broad gauge locomotives ever operated, from the first *Vulcan* to the latest *Fire Fly* replica. Not just those of the Great Western Railway and the "Associated Companies", but also those of the independent lines such as the North Devon Railway, and of the industrial concerns and railway contractors. It is unlikely that we will ever fully understand the history of many of these smaller operators, and so there are no doubt gaps and inaccuracies in their lists. Even among the GWR records the same locomotive can be found with conflicting information and we may never see the true picture.

Dates given are generally those when a locomotive was in service on the broad gauge. The building or withdrawal dates of converted locomotives in their narrow gauge form is outside the scope of this book, however these are identified by a © before the date. Those significantly rebuilt, such as a tender locomotive rebuilt as a tank, are marked with an ® before the date. Many locomotives were recorded as cut up many months before or after they were officially taken out of stock so the WDN (withdrawn) dates shown use the earlier of these two dates when both are known. The picture is all the more confusing as the records seldom show the exact day of a locomotive being delivered or withdrawn, but rather a period which may cover a fortnight, four weeks, or half year. For instance, the first *Alma* (A17) is recorded as started in 11/54 and condemned 6/72, although according to another list it had been dismantled and used as stationary boiler since 2/72. A "renewed" *Alma* (A18) was then "taken into rebuilding" during the two weeks ended 28/6/1879 and was condemned during the four weeks ended 14/5/1892.

The names given to locomotive classes are often just conveniences used by historians as the railway companies often just classified locomotives as "passenger" or "goods" or by the size of its driving wheels; the GWR combined all of its locomotives in 1866 into just 14 classes which are used in this book where appropriate. This book uses the alpha-numeric classification system originally devised for the Broad Gauge Society Image Database to allow quick identification of a locomotive type within all the different fleets. The letter of this identifies the original company (A for Great Western; B for Bristol & Exeter; D for South Devon; C for all the smaller operators and contractors). The first digit generally shows the number of driving wheels, for example A17 is a GWR single-driver tender locomotive while B42 is a B&ER four-coupled tank. Named locomotives are generally shown within their class in the order delivered but numbered locomotives are shown in numerical order.

The wheel arrangement is shown using the modern Whyte notation system but this does not clearly reflect some of the more unusual locomotives, and it should be noted that most of the 4-2-2 locomotives did not have a leading bogie, the leading axles being carried in the same frames as the driving and trailing wheels.

The first details of broad gauge locomotives were published in magazines more than a century ago. Lists of GWR locomotives were published later by the GWR and RCTS but these books are now long out of print, while Laurence Waters' more recent and copiously illustrated book does not have the detailed lists of locomotives that appeared in the earlier works. Much of the original information for these books came from records that are now held in The National Archive at Kew and these have been consulted in writing this current book, in particular a list of locomotives dated 1866 (RAIL 254/37), a locomotive stock book showing details of most disposals (RAIL 254/148), and the returns of locomotives from 1877 (RAIL 254/142 & 143). Our knowledge of the broad gauge has increased tremendously since the formation of the Broad Gauge Society (BGS) in 1980 and use has been made of research by several BGS members, most of which has been published its *Broadsheet* journal. Special thanks must go to Brian Arman and Paul Garnsworthy who have contributed many of the railway histories and notes on individual locomotives. Paul also painted the illustration on the front cover, while the photographs have been drawn from the collections of the BGS and several of its members.

Geof Sheppard

Broad gauge locomotives in 2008

NAME	BUILT	TYPE	STATUS	LOCATION
Tiny	1868	D50 0-4-0vb	On display	Buckfastleigh
2	1883	C97 0-4-0ST	Stored	Ponta Delgada
3	1888	C97 0-4-0ST	Stored	Ponta Delgada
North Star	1925	A91 2-2-2	On display	Swindon
Iron Duke	1985	A91 4-2-2	On display	York
Fire Fly	2005	A91 2-2-2	In service	Didcot

Above - The first locomotive shed was situated at Paddington, a 130ft wooden roundhouse to which a through shed was later added. When the station was rebuilt new facilities were provided a little further down the line at Westbourne Park where a 663ft brick-built through shed spanned four tracks. Parallel to this was a 110ft long two-road repair shed. Further facilities were added at a later date for narrow gauge locomotives and some of the broad gauge shed was converted for their use, but broad gauge locomotives were serviced here right up to the end of the broad gauge. On the weekend before the gauge conversion there were nine based here, compared with 33 in steam in 1860.

The photograph shows Alma class Great Britain (A18) standing in front of the small shed after it had been rebuilt in 1870. Several other photographs in this book (A17, A18, A57) were taken to the right of this spot with Alfred Villa, the superintendent's house, in the background.

Above - The GWR reached Weymouth on 20 January 1857 and this photograph was taken within a few years of opening. The locomotive facilities were provided a short distance outside the station on the east side of the line. The two-track shed, which was about 130ft long, was approached across a 35ft turntable which is just out of this view. In 1860 five locomotives were in steam here each day.

Opposite - The Bristol & Exeter Railway opened their main locomotive facility at Bristol in 1850. The impressive workshops stood alongside their main line between the bridge over the New Cut of the River Avon and the one that carried the Bath Road over the line. The rail entrance to the workshops was through the arch beneath the clock seen behind Swallow (A18). The old carriages are pilot vans that were used to deal with derailments and other incidents, and they can be seen again in the photograph of number 1204 (A59). Behind the tender is the main running shed. In 1877 the GWR closed its nearby shed at South Wales Junction and converted the B&ER workshops to house narrow gauge locomotives, but 32 broad gauge locomotives were still based here in 1892.

Almost every branch line had its own shed, generally at the terminus but occasionally at the junction with the main line. Typical facilities would comprise a building large enough for one or two locomotives, an office, water tower and coal store. A turntable was invariably provided, even if all trains were worked by tank locomotives. At Launceston the turntable was immediately outside the shed doors, as can be seen in the picture of Dragon (D65). The shed in this picture is at Farringdon, and it was photographed in 1868 with Aries, a Leo tank **(A41)**, posed outside

The South Devon Railway built a shed outside its Plymouth Millbay terminus, but both the station and locomotive facilities were expanded to accommodate the arrival of the Cornwall Railway in 1859. A 190ft four-road shed was alongside the running lines and a 145ft two-road shed was built on additional ground to the west. In 1876 there were 22 tank locomotives here. A lifting shop was added behind the old shed in 1884 and a larger turntable was installed which then allowed tender locomotives to be turned without running up to the triangle at North Road. This picture, taken about 1890, finds a 1076 class 0-6-0ST (A64) inside the small shed with three more locomotives standing outside the large shed: 3501 class 2-4-0T (A45) number 3505, another 1076 class, and a former B&ER 4-4-0ST (B43).

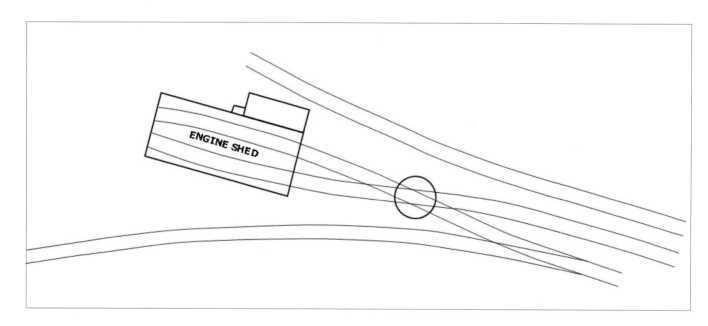

A shed was opened at Truro in 1859 beside the then terminus of the Cornwall Railway. It was a wooden building, reported by the local paper as 100ft long and 45ft wide, which spanned two tracks. It was provided with a smithy but saw less use after the line was extended to Falmouth in 1863. In 1876 it was home to just three locomotives.

The history of the Great Western Railway's broad gauge locomotive policy and development can conveniently be divided into three periods: development; standardisation, and decline.

Development

It is well known that Isambard Kingdom Brunel drew up the early specification for the first locomotives ordered for the GWR. He required that piston speed should not exceed 280ft per minute at 30 mph, and that the weight of the six-wheeled locomotive specified should not exceed 10½ tons. To comply with these stringent regulations four of the five different makers were forced to produce locomotives with small boilers and very large driving wheels (A11). However, TE Harrison of R&W Hawthorn & Co developed patent locomotives with the boiler and engine on different carriages (A01, A02) so, in a sense, foreshadowing the work of Mallet and Beyer Peacock & Co, but rather less successfully! To add to the problems some of the locomotives, especially those of Mather Dixon, were poorly constructed which did not add to their usefulness.

Brunel has been and continues to be excoriated for setting these specifications, and certainly the locomotives built for the GWR in 1837 and 1838 were largely failures which caused Daniel Gooch, the first locomotive superintendent, many sleepless nights as his diary vividly bears out. But we must recall that Brunel was working at the cutting edge of technology with untested permanent way and the then constant problem for locomotive engineers of lubrication. There were no lubricating oils of any kind available then, tallow (animal fat) alone being in universal use. It might well be these considerations which caused Brunel to issue such restricting specifications. Neither should we forget that many early railways experienced chronic problems with the locomotives of more conventional design with which they were supplied, so the well-documented problems of the GWR were far from unique, if rather of their own making.

Standardisation

Brunel may have been in error in laying down the early specifications for the GWR's motive power but he made no mistake when he appointed Daniel Gooch, still only 20 years of age, as the company's first locomotive superintendent. At the time of his appointment Gooch was aware that Robert Stephenson & Co had two locomotives for sale at their Newcastle works. Gooch persuaded the GWR Board to purchase these locomotives (A12) which were of a robust double-framed construction and carried a much larger boiler than those built to Brunel's inadequate specifications. The now almost legendary *North Star* hauled the first GWR train, a directors' special, on 31 May 1838. With her sister *Morning Star*, these two locomotives were far and away the most reliable in the company's service at this time.

Gooch, whose own reputation was at stake, saw their potential and set to designing a group of standard locomotives that would draw upon the lessons learned during those early, difficult days. Working in close collaboration with his chief draughtsman, Thomas Crampton, a series of four standard types of locomotives were envisaged, all with slotted sandwich frames, adequate boilers, and fitted with haycock fireboxes (coke was universal at this time rather than coal). Not only did Gooch carefully lay down all the relevant dimensions, he had templates made which could be distributed to the various locomotive builders to ensure standardisation of parts to facilitate subsequent interchange of components. His four types, 7ft and 6ft passenger (A13 & A14), four-coupled and six-coupled goods (A31 & A51), set up the GWR for the next decade of development and rapidly transformed its somewhat precarious reputation for reliability into that of the foremost railway in the land.

In 1845 the Government set up a Gauge Commission to investigate the vexed question of a future standard track gauge. For these trials Gooch designed *Great Western* (A16), an enlarged Fire Fly with 8ft driving wheels and a much enlarged boiler. This locomotive has the distinction of being the first locomotive completely constructed at Swindon Works, some earlier goods locomotives of the Premier class (A53) had been built there but with boilers supplied by R Stephenson & Co. *Great Western* broke her leading axle after a few months of running and was rebuilt with two leading axles and thus became a prototype for Gooch's *magnum opus*, his Alma class of 1847 (A17). These were, at the time, among the largest locomotives in the world and certainly the speediest. They were of the 4-2-2 type with 8ft driving wheels and 18in x 24in cylinders. The same basic design, although much improved, served the GWR until the abolition of the broad gauge in May 1892.

In 1848 Gooch, under the GWR, became responsible for supplying motive power to the South Devon Railway following the abandonment of the atmospheric system, and for this concern he designed the first true swivelling bogie and applied it to a neat 4-4-0ST design (A42) of which two were built in 1849. He went on to design both 4-4-0 (without a bogie; A32) and 2-4-0 (A33) tender classes for use on the South Wales Railway and the Wilts, Somerset & Weymouth Railway. Between 1846 and 1863 129 0-6-0 tender locomotives (A57) were constructed to the same basic design with inside sandwich frames of ever lengthening wheelbases, increasingly large boilers and cylinders.

Gooch's last design broke with his previous practice for he built a batch of 22 2-4-0STs (A43) for working the Metropolitan Railway. They had solid plate frames, outside cylinders, and condensing gear. These were always poor performers and quickly rendered redundant when the GWR and Metropolitan fell out. Some of them, even after conversion to tender locomotives, lasted less than ten years in traffic.

In 1843 Gooch introduced a form of stationary link motion to replace the old Gab motion or valve gear of the earliest designs. In 1848 he also designed and built what was probably the first dynamometer car in the world for purposes of estimating train resistance at various speeds. He retired as the GWR's locomotive superintendent in September 1864.

Decline

Joseph Armstrong, locomotive superintendent from 1864 to

1877, is one of the GWR's unsung heroes. He built solid, reliable locomotives with rugged plate frames and fitted Stephenson link motion as standard. He contributed three classes of pure broad gauge locomotives: the Hawthorn class 2-4-0s of 1865 (A35), some of which were later converted to saddle tanks (A44); the Swindon class of fourteen 0-6-0 goods locomotives in 1865-6 (A58); and six 0-6-0Ts fitted with condensing gear for working goods trains on the Metropolitan Railway (A63). This small class had the distinction of being the last new design of purely broad gauge locomotives built for the GWR.

In 1870 Armstrong made a start at renewing the earlier Gooch singles of the Alma class by extending their wheelbase and giving them new cylinders and larger boiler (A18). The first few so treated were probably genuine rebuilds but later locomotives were wholly new replacements of their illustrious forebears.

In 1876 Armstrong built a batch of ten 0-6-0STs to his standard narrow gauge design but with broad gauge wheels set outside the plate frames (A64). By 1875 the GWR had become essentially a narrow gauge railway with the broad gauge only retained on the Windsor, Henley and Farringdon branches, and for through running to the South West. In 1876, however, the GWR amalgamated with the Bristol & Exeter and South Devon railways. The GWR thus acquired 180 broad gauge locomotives, some of which were in urgent need of replacement.

William Dean continued his predecessor's renewal programme for the Almas, and the work of providing convertible locomotives. These were the 0-6-0 type, both saddle tank (A64) and tender locomotives (A59) of basically similar designs. He also built convertible locomotives intended for passenger work west of Newton Abbot. Ten 2-4-0Ts (A45) were followed by a class of 0-4-2STs (A46) that proved unsteady at speed; the last built was turned out as an 0-4-4T (A47) and the rest were rebuilt accordingly. He also built an experimental four-cylinder tandem-compound (A36), number 8, which did little if any useful work, and two rather handsome 2-4-0 locomotives (A37), 14 & 16, especially for work between Swindon and Bristol as the heaviest passenger trains were becoming too much for the Alma Class singles. Finally, in 1891, eight locomotives of the 7ft 6in single-wheel design were built as convertibles (A19) and were intended, on conversion, to replace the Alma Class on the best trains. As a stop gap in 1888 he had built three new Almas which had the distinction of being the last purely broad gauge locomotives produced for the GWR.

Absorbed locomotives

The 19 Vale of Neath Railway locomotives (C11-C17) were transferred to the GWR at the end of 1866. In January 1870 there were 419 locomotives in stock but the conversion of many of the GWR's broad gauge lines to narrow gauge over the next few years allowed the withdrawal of most of the earlier locomotives.

Things changed in 1876 with the arrival of 95 Bristol & Exeter Railway locomotives (A58, B11-B63) in January; and 85 from the South Devon Railway (A61, A62, C22, C26, D41-D66) the following month. The older specimens were withdrawn before the end of the year, leaving 260 locomotives in stock. By May 1892, when the last broad gauge trains ran, the stock had been reduced to 195. Most of these were convertible locomotives built during the previous 16 years.

The B&ER added 47 tenders to the GWR's stock, taking the sequential numbering to 368, although tenders do not appear to have been allocated numbers until sometime after 1866. They were kept much longer than locomotives, being passed from withdrawn locomotives to new ones. Some had just four wheels but six-wheel tenders were prevalent.

Livery

There is much dispute about the early liveries in use, especially the colour of the lining employed.

Up to 1848

A specification of 1842 calls for the frames to be painted chocolate brown; frame ties, steps, springs, smokebox, boiler brackets, chimney and other ferrous fittings: black; splashers and handrails were polished brass or steel; wheels were dark holly green with black tyres; and the boiler, which was lagged with wooden strips, was painted dark holly green with black boiler bands. Buffer beams and the inside of the frames were vermillion. Some of the earlier locomotives probably had the slatted boiler lagging polished rather than painted.

1848 to 1881

In 1848 the 4-2-2 (A17) *Courier* was turned out with the wood lagging sheeted over and painted holly green. Tenders followed the general specification for the locomotives and were lined out, possibly initially with straw-coloured lining which by the early 1860s had become pea green edged with white and black. 'Straw' and 'pea green' might well describe the same basic colour which perhaps changed subtly in hue.

A further specification of 1865 similarly stipulates: "Boilers to have four coats of red lead before cladding. Cladding plates to be painted two coats of red lead inside. The locomotive and tender when finished to have four coats [of presumably red lead, the specification is rather vague]… The boiler and the wheels to be green and the frames brown, picked out with red and black – a sample of each colour will be supplied to the manufacturer." No tender lining is mentioned though a tender was included in the specification, perhaps lining was added at Swindon on delivery of the finished locomotive? Indeed this may have been intended since no lining of the locomotive is mentioned except on the frame.

Opposite - 2-2-2 *Ajax* **(A11)** was built by Mather, Dixon and delivered on 12 December 1838. In some respects it is a controversial locomotive and many dimensions are uncertain, however this drawing by Lane depicts it here is the best possible construction of the details known to us. Its major feature are the 10ft plated driving wheels, these were possibly replaced by wheels of 8ft diameter with correspondingly smaller carrying wheels but this is not known for sure. It ceased work in June 1840 but was still extant in 1849.

By the early 1870s boiler bands were edged with white. Buffer beams and the inside of the frames remained vermillion but were now edged in black picked out with white lining. Coupling rods were brown with polished bosses. In 1876 the deep copper-topped bell-mouth chimneys were replaced by the roll-top chimneys and the majority of broad gauge locomotives were fitted with these. Domes, where applied, were painted.

1881 to 1892

In 1881 the whole painting scheme changed. The green became slightly lighter and frames were deep Indian red.

Locomotives and tenders were lined out with the familiar black bands edged in chrome-orange. Until 1886 wheels remained green but then wheels were painted Indian red to match the frames and wheel bosses were lined black and orange. Coupling rods were polished, as was all brightwork. Smokeboxes, running plates, chimneys, cab roofs, etc. remained black while buffer beams and the inside of frames remained vermillion. In 1880 the shallow and elegant copper-capped chimney replaced the roll-top pattern and domes, especially on the convertible locomotives, became far more common and were polished.

A01	Thunderer	0-4-0+6

TOTAL: 1   PERIOD: 1838-39
BUILDER: R & W Hawthorn
CYLINDERS: 16in x 20in
DRIVING WHEELS: 6ft 0in
CARRYING WHEELS: 4ft 6in / 4ft 0in

NAME	NEW	WDN	
Thunderer	3/38	12/39	①

① *Boiler and engine carried on separate frames. Driving wheels geared 27:10.*

A02	Hurricane	2-2-2+6

TOTAL: 1   PERIOD: 1838-39
BUILDER: R & W Hawthorn
CYLINDERS: 16in x 20in
DRIVING WHEELS: 10ft 0in
CARRYING WHEELS: 4ft 6in?

NAME	NEW	WDN	
Hurricane	10/38	12/39	①

① *Boiler and engine carried on separate frames. Some parts used to construct 0-6-0 Bacchus (A55).*

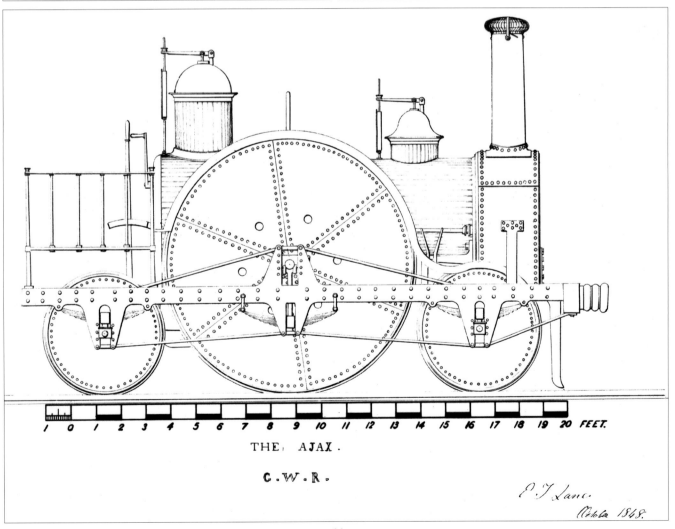

THE AJAX.

G.W.R.

A11   2-2-2

TOTAL: 17   PERIOD: 1837-47

BUILDER: Mather, Dixon (MD), Charles Tayleur (CT), Sharp Roberts (SR), Haigh Foundry (HF)

NAME	NEW	WDN	BUILDER	CYLINDERS	WHEELS	
Premier	11/37	12/40	MD	14½in x 14½in	7ft 0in + 4ft 6in	
Aeolus	11/37	® c.1846	CT	14in x 16in	8ft 0in + 4ft 6in	①
Bacchus	12/37	1842	CT	14in x 16in	8ft 0in + 4ft 6in	②
Apollo	1/38	® c.1846	CT	12in x 16 in	8ft 0in + 4ft 6in	①②
Vulcan	1/38	® 12/43	CT	14in x 16in	8ft 0in + 4ft 6in	②③
Neptune	1/38	6/40	CT	12in x 16 in	8ft 0in + 4ft 6in	
Ariel	3/38	12/40	MD	14in x 14in	7ft 0in + 4ft 6in	
Lion	5/38	6/47	SR	14in x 15in	6ft 0in + 3ft 6in	
Atlas	6/38	®	SR	14in x 15in	6ft 0in + 3ft 6in	
Venus	8/38	® 1843	CT	12in x 16 in	8ft 0in + 4ft 6in	①⑤
Viper	8/38	®	HF	15in x 18in	6ft 0in + 4ft 6in	④
Snake	9/38	®	HF	15in x 18in	6ft 0in + 4ft 6in	④
Eagle	11/38	®	SR	14in x 15in	6ft 0in + 3ft 6in	
Ajax	12/38	6/40	MD	14in x 20in	8ft 0in + 4ft 0in	⑤
Planet	8/39	6/40	MD	16in x 20in	8ft 0in + 4ft 0in	
Mercury	9/39	12/43	MD	16in x 20in	8ft 0in + 4ft 0in	⑥
Mars	4/40	12/40	MD	16in x 20in	8ft 0in + 4ft 0in	⑤

®   Rebuilt locomotives became 2-2-2STs, see A23, A24 and A25.

① Apollo was rebuilt with 6ft 0in driving wheels, 3ft 0in carrying wheels and 15in x 18in cylinders from 1839, Aeolus was the same from 1843. Venus was in this condition by the time it was converted to a tank locomotive 1846

② Aeolus, Bacchus and Vulcan were built with 14in x 16in cylinders.

③ Vulcan was delivered on 25 November 1837 and was tested in steam on 28 December, but is recorded as entering service in January 1838.

④ Snake and Viper were delivered with 14¾in cylinders and 6ft 4in wheels geared 3:2. They were rebuilt in conventional form with 13in x 18in cylinders in 1839-40 but later recorded with 15in. x 18in cylinders. They carried the names **Teign** (Viper) and **Exe** (Snake) from 1846 to 1851 for working trains on the SDR

⑤ Ajax and Mars were originally built with 10ft 0in driving wheels, Mars was certainly altered before entering service. Carrying wheels may have been 5ft 0in.

⑥   Mercury was later recorded with 14in x 18in cylinders.

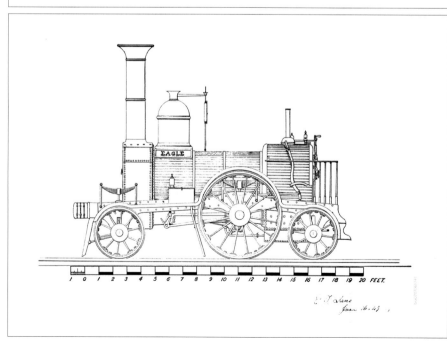

2-2-2 Eagle (A11) was delivered on 8 November 1838 and was built by Sharp, Roberts of Manchester, the third of three locomotives of more conventional design. Following rebuilding in December 1860 as a 2-2-2ST with larger cylinders and a new boiler, it ceased work in December 1871.

A12		Priam class	2-2-2

TOTAL: 12   PERIOD: 1837-71
BUILDER: R Stephenson & Co
CYLINDERS: See below
DRIVING WHEELS: 7ft 0in (② 6ft 6in)
CARRYING WHEELS: 4ft 0in

NAME	NEW	WDN	CYLINDERS	
North Star	11/37	12/70	16in x 16in	①
Morning Star	1/39	11/69	16in x 16in	②
Evening Star	7/39	6/71	15in x 18in	
Dog Star	9/39	1869	15in x 18in	
Polar Star	7/40	®	15½in x 18in	
Red Star	8/40	®	15in x 18in	
Load Star	1/41	7/70	15in x 18in	
Rising Star	3/41	®	15in x 18in	
Bright Star	4/41	®	15in x 18in	
Shooting Star	8/41	®	15in x 18in	
Royal Star	11/41	1/69	15½in x 19in	
Western Star	11/41	10/66	15½in x 19in	

® *Rebuilt locomotives became 4-2-2STs c.1849, see A21.*

① *North Star was recorded as a Wolf class 4-2-2 tank locomotive but there is no visible evidence of any side or saddle tank being fitted. It was stored at Swindon after withdrawal until dismantled in 1906.*

② *Morning Star had 6ft 6in driving wheels.*

North Star (A12), a 2-2-2 built by Robert Stephenson & Co and delivered on 20 November 1837, is one of the most famous locomotives in the world; it hauled the first directors' special on 31 May 1838. The Stars were by far and away the best locomotives with which the GWR began operations and formed a kind of prototype for many of its future designs. Despite the fact that contemporary lists include North Star with the Wolf class tank locomotives, there is no evidence that this conversion took place. A well tank may have been fitted between the frames but the locomotive retained its original small tender. On withdrawal it was preserved at Swindon and, along with Lord of the Isles (A17), was sent to the international exhibition at Chicago in 1893. Despite attempts to place it in the Science Museum and, failing that, on a plinth in New Swindon, it was finally broken up in 1906. Fortunately many parts were hidden away in Swindon Works and re-emerged in 1925 when the present replica was built. This photograph shows it in 1871 when it ceased work, whereas the replica illustrates the locomotive in its original form.

A13		Priam class		2-2-2

TOTAL: 62   PERIOD: 1840-78
BUILDER: Fenton, Murray & Jackson (FMJ), Jones, Turner &
Evans (JTE), R B Longridge & Co (RBL), Nasmyth, Gaskell &
Co (NG),G & J Rennie (Ren), Sharp, Roberts & Co (SR),
Stothert & Slaughter (SS)
CYLINDERS: 15in x 18in or 15¾in x 18in; fitted with 16in x 20in
from 1844
DRIVING WHEELS: 7ft 0in
CARRYING WHEELS: 4ft 0in

NAME	BUILDER	NEW	WDN
Tiger	SR	4/40	12/73

Spit Fire	JTE	4/40	10/78
Wild Fire	JTE	4/40	7/67
Leopard	SR	5/40	11/78
Fire Ball	JTE	5/40	®
Fire King	JTE	5/40	®
Fire Brand	JTE	5/40	4/66
Fire Fly	JTE	5/40	7/70
Charon	FMJ	5/40	6/78
Panther	SR	6/40	12/69
Lynx	SR	7/40	12/70
Stag	SR	9/40	12/63

The Fire Fly series 2-2-2 locomotives such as Actaeon (A13) were designed by Daniel Gooch in 1840 and were a direct development of the Stephenson Stars of 1837. They were built in different batches by no less than seven different manufacturers, this one in December 1841 by Nasmyth, Gaskell & Co of Manchester. In their day they were the best locomotives in the country and were responsible for working many of the first trains as the line between London and Exeter opened progressively, as well as taking a leading role in the gauge disputes. From 1847 they were eclipsed by the 8ft 4-2-2s (A17) but they continued to work, particularly on the South Wales and the Wilt, Somerset and Weymouth railways, until the conversion of those lines. Actaeon's boiler exploded at Gloucester in February 1855, and as a result it was the first of the type to be renewed. It ceased work in March 1868 after which it became a stationary boiler at Newport. The last of the type was withdrawn from ordinary service in 1879.

2-2-2 Saturn (A13) built by Longridge & Co in June 1841 and shown here at Gloucester following renewal with lengthened frames, new cylinders, boiler and cab in October 1864. It ceased work in June 1878 when its boiler was sold to the Metropolitan Board of Works for further use.

Hawk	SR	10/40	12/65
Vulture	SR	10/40	12/70
Cyclops	FMJ	10/40	5/65
Falcon	SR	11/40	12/67
Ostrich	SR	12/40	12/65
Greyhound	SR	1/41	6/66
Mazeppa	Ren	3/41	3/68
Arab	Ren	4/41	7/70
Jupiter	RBL	4/41	6/67
Cerebus	FMJ	6/41	2/66
Achilles	NG	6/41	4/67
Milo	NG	6/41	2/66
Saturn	RBL	6/41	6/78
Arrow	SS	7/41	12/64
Dart	SS	7/41	12/70
Hector	NG	7/41	11/66
Mars	RBL	7/41	9/68
Harpy	FMJ	8/41	6/73
Pluto	FMJ	8/41	7/70
Castor	NG	8/41	6/74
Mentor	NG	8/41	11/67
Lucifer	RBL	8/41	5/70
Minos	FMJ	9/41	7/70
Ixion	FMJ	10/41	2/79
Mercury	RBL	10/41	2/65
Venus	RBL	10/41	7/70
Gorgon	FMJ	11/41	10/78
Hecate	FMJ	11/41	4/67
Bellona	NG	11/41	7/70
Vesta	FMJ	12/41	12/64
Actaeon	NG	12/41	3/68
Centaur	NG	12/41	11/67

Acheron	FMJ	1/42	2/66
Erebus	FMJ	2/42	6/73
Medea	FMJ	3/42	12/73
Damon	NG	3/42	6/70
Electra	NG	3/42	1/67
Orion	NG	3/42	®
Priam	NG	3/42	6/64
Lethe	FMJ	4/42	10/78
Hydra	FMJ	4/42	6/65
Phlegethon	FMJ	5/42	1/66
Medusa	FMJ	6/42	10/64
Proserpine	FMJ	6/42	6/73
Ganymede	FMJ	7/42	8/78
Pollux	NG	7/42	2/66
Argus	FMJ	8/42	6/73
Phoenix	NG	8/42	12/69
Pegasus	NG	12/42	6/68
Stentor	NG	12/42	4/68

® c.1849 Fire Ball and Fire King became 2-2-2STs, see A24, and Orion became a 2-2-2ST, see A21.

A14	Sun class	2-2-2

TOTAL: 21   PERIOD: 1840-49
BUILDER: R & W Hawthorn (Haw), Sharp, Roberts (SR),
            Stothert & Slaughter (SS)
CYLINDERS: 14in x 18in (②15in x 18in)
DRIVING WHEELS: 6ft 0in
CARRYING WHEELS: 3ft 6in

NAME	NEW	WDN	
Sun	4/40	Ⓡ	Haw
Sunbeam	5/40	Ⓡ	Haw
Eclipse	8/40	Ⓡ	Haw
Meridian	8/40	Ⓡ	Haw
Comet	10/40	Ⓡ	Haw ①
Meteor	11/40	Ⓡ	Haw
Aurora	12/40	Ⓡ	Haw ①
Hesperus	1/41	Ⓡ	Haw ①②
Gazelle	3/41	Ⓡ	SR
Wolf	7/41	Ⓡ	SR
Djerid	7/41	Ⓡ	SS
Javelin	7/41	Ⓡ	SS
Antelope	8/41	Ⓡ	SR
Zebra	8/41	Ⓡ	SR
Lance	8/41	Ⓡ	SS
Yataghan	8/41	Ⓡ	SS
Giraffe	9/41	Ⓡ	SR
Assagais	9/41	Ⓡ	SS
Rocket	11/41	Ⓡ	SS
Stiletto	12/41	Ⓡ	SS
Creese	6/42	Ⓡ	SS

Ⓡ *All locomotives rebuilt as 2-2-2ST c.1849, see A24.*
① *Comet, Aurora and Hesperus had 15in x 18in cylinders.*
② *Hesperus was built with an experimental boiler and firebox with return tubes; it was rebuilt as a conventional locomotive.*

A15 Priam class 2-2-2

TOTAL: 6   PERIOD: 1846-71
BUILDER: Great Western Railway
CYLINDERS: 16in x 24in
DRIVING WHEELS: 7ft 0in (① 7ft 6in)
CARRYING WHEELS: 4ft 0in

NAME	NEW	WDN	
Elk	8/46	9/70	
Prince	8/46	6/70	
Peri	11/46	7/70	
Witch	12/46	6/71	①
Queen	2/47	1/70	
Sylph	3/47	4/70	

① *Witch was fitted with 7ft 6in driving wheels.*

A16 Great Western 2-2-2

TOTAL: 1   PERIOD: 1846
BUILDER: Great Western Railway
CYLINDERS: 18in x 24in
DRIVING WHEELS: 8ft 0in
CARRYING WHEELS: 4ft 6in

NAME	NEW	WDN
Great Western	4/46	Ⓡ

Ⓡ *Rebuilt as 4-2-2, see A17*

2-2-2 Prince was one of the 7ft singles (A15) built at Swindon in 1846 and 1847. These were produced as a stop gap whilst trials proceeded with the 8ft 2-2-2 Great Western. For a short time they worked the major expresses to Exeter but were soon replaced and subsequently saw extensive use on the new line to Birmingham. All six ceased work in 1870. In later years all the 7ft singles, including Stars, Fire Flys and Princes, were known as the Priam class.

*Sultan was one of the iconic 8ft 4-2-2s designed by Daniel Gooch **(A17)** and built in batches between 1847 and 1855, the majority at Swindon but the last seven by Rothwell & Co. Unquestionably the most advanced locomotives in the world at the time of their construction, they served the broad gauge faithfully until its demise in 1892. Sultan was built in November 1847 and, in the original condition seen here at Westbourne Park in London circa 1860, worked until June 1874 having run an 727,300 miles. It was then replaced by a new locomotive that carried the same name that went into service in September 1876.*

A17	Alma class	4-4-2

BUILDER: Great Western Railway (③Rothwell & Co)
CYLINDERS: 18in x 24in
DRIVING WHEELS: 8ft 0in
CARRYING WHEELS: 4ft 6in (See ①)

NAME	NEW	WDN	
Great Western	®	12/70	①
Iron Duke	4/47	10/71	
Great Britain	7/47	7/70	
Lightning	8/47	12/77	
Emperor	9/47	6/73	
Sultan	11/47	6/74	
Pasha	11/47	6/76	
Courier	6/48	11/77	
Tartar	7/48	6/76	
Dragon	8/48	12/72	
Warlock	8/48	6/74	
Wizard	9/48	11/75	
Rougemount	10/48	8/79	
Hirondelle	12/48	2/72	
Tornado	3/49	6/81	
Swallow	6/49	8/71	
Timour	8/49	11/71	
Prometheus	3/50	6/70	
Perseus	6/50	2/80	
Estaffete	9/50	6/70	
Rover	9/50	8/71	
Amazon	3/51	6/77	
Lord of the Isles	3/51	6/84	②
Alma	11/54	2/72	③
Balaklava	12/54	10/71	③
Inkermann	3/55	7/77	③
Kertch	4/55	12/72	③
Crimea	5/55	11/76	③
Eupatoria	5/55	10/78	③
Sebastopol	7/55	6/80	③

① Great Western originally ran as a 2-2-2, see A16. It was recorded at different times with either 4ft 0in or 4ft 1in carrying wheels and 4ft 7in training wheels.

② Lord of the Isles was built in March 1851 and exhibited at the Great Exhibition as **Charles Russell**, although it did not enter service until 7/52 by which time it had been renamed. It was kept as an exhibition locomotive after withdrawal until dismantled in February 1906.

③ The final batch of seven locomotives was built by Rothwell & Co.

A18	Alma class		4-2-2

TOTAL: 25   PERIOD: 1870-92
BUILDER: Great Western Railway
CYLINDERS: 18in x 24in
DRIVING WHEELS: 8ft 0in
CARRYING WHEELS: 4ft 6in

NAME	NEW	WDN	
Estaffete	6/70	12/84	
Prometheus	6/70	5/92	
Great Britain	7/70	5/92	
Rover	8/71	5/92	
Swallow	9/71	5/92	
Balaklava	10/71	5/92	
Hirondelle	5/73	12/90	
Timour	7/73	5/92	
Iron Duke	8/73	5/92	
Tartar	8/76	5/92	
Sultan	9/76	5/92	
Warlock	12/76	5/92	
Lightning	9/78	5/92	
Amazon	10/78	5/92	
Crimea	10/78	5/92	
Eupatoria	11/78	5/92	
Inkermann	11/78	5/92	
Courier	11/78	5/92	①
Bulkeley	7/80	5/92	
Dragon	10/80	5/92	
Emperor	11/80	5/92	
Sebastopol	12/80	5/92	
Alma	11/80	5/92	①
Great Western	5/88	5/92	
Tornado	8/88	5/92	

① *Alma and Courier ceased running before the gauge conversion weekend.*

A19	3001 class		2-2-2

TOTAL: 8   PERIOD: 1891-92
BUILDER: Great Western Railway
CYLINDERS: 20in x 24in
DRIVING WHEELS: 7ft 8½in
CARRYING WHEELS: 4ft 7in

NUMBER	NEW	WDN
3021	3/91	Ⓒ 5/92
3022	7/91	Ⓒ 5/92
3023	8/91	Ⓒ 5/92
3024	9/91	Ⓒ 5/92
3025	9/91	Ⓒ 5/92
3026	9/91	Ⓒ 5/92
3027	10/91	Ⓒ 5/92
3028	10/91	Ⓒ 5/92

A21	Wolf class		4-2-2ST

TOTAL: 6   PERIOD: c.1849-71
BUILDER: Rebuilt from 2-2-2, see A12
CYLINDERS: 15in x 18in
DRIVING WHEELS: 7ft 0in
CARRYING WHEELS: 4ft 0in (③ 3ft 6in)

NAME	NEW	WDN	
North Star			①
Orion	Ⓡ	11/69	②
Bright Star	Ⓡ	4/64	
Polar Star	Ⓡ	7/70	
Red Star	Ⓡ	2/65	③
Rising Star	Ⓡ	11/66	
Shooting Star	Ⓡ	6/71	

① *North Star was stored at Swindon after withdrawal until dismantled in 1906. It was classified as a Wolf class 4-2-2 tank locomotive but there is no visible evidence of any side or saddle tank being fitted.*

② *Orion was rebuilt from a Fire Fly series locomotive, see A13.*

③ *Red Star was recorded with 3ft 6in carrying wheels.*

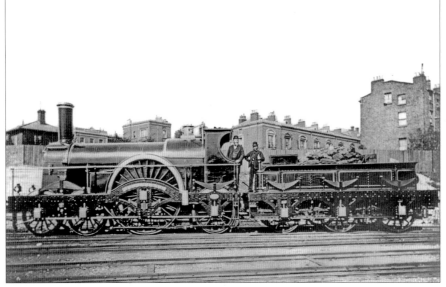

8ft 4-2-2s, both original locomotives and renewals (A18) such as Eupatoria, officially became known as the Alma class. The original Eupatoria was built by Rothwell & Co in May 1855 but was replaced in October 1878 by the new locomotive pictured here, again at Westbourne Park. These renewals were constructed in small batches, each one differing slightly from its predecessor. Eupatoria was one of six locomotives built in 1878 and in our photograph it is shown in its original condition with Armstrong rolled chimney and scafed pea-green lining. The 1880 and 1888 batches, numbering nine locomotives, together with three earlier locomotives which were rebuilt a second time, carried slightly larger boilers and were finished with the more handsome Dean lipped chimney and the new lighter green livery with chrome and black lining. By 1885 the remaining locomotives on the class had been brought up to date, and all save Hirondelle worked until 1892.

During the final thirteen months of operation the Almas were supplemented by eight 7ft 8½in 2-2-2s of the narrow gauge 3021 class fitted with broad gauge wheels and tenders (A19). 3026 was turned out in August 1891, ran on the broad gauge until May 1892, and was working narrow gauge trains by July that year.

A23	Wolf class	2-2-2ST

TOTAL: 1   PERIOD: 1846?-70
BUILDER: Rebuilt from 2-2-2, see A11
CYLINDERS: 15in x 18in
DRIVING WHEELS: 6ft 0in
CARRYING WHEELS: 4ft 0in

NAME	NEW	WDN
Venus	℞ 1846?	7/70

A24	Wolf class	2-2-2ST

TOTAL: 27   PERIOD: c.1849-76
BUILDER: Rebuilt from 2-2-2, see A14, (① A11), (② A13)
CYLINDERS: 15in x 18in
DRIVING WHEELS: 6ft 0in
CARRYING WHEELS: 3ft 6in

NAME	NEW	WDN	
Antelope	℞	7/70	
Assagais	℞	6/75	
Atlas	℞ 7/60	6/72	①
Aurora	℞	12/66	
Comet	℞	6/71	

Creese	℞	3/66	
Djerid	℞	7/70	
Eagle	℞ 12/60	12/71	①
Eclipse	℞	6/64	
Fire Ball	℞	10/66	②
Fire King	℞	6/75	②
Gazelle	℞	6/79	
Giraffe	℞	3/72	
Hesperus	℞	8/76	
Javelin	℞	9/70	
Lance	℞	11/70	
Meridian	℞	8/70	
Meteor	℞	1/64	
Rocket	℞	7/70	
Snake	℞	11/69	①
Stiletto	℞	1/70	
Sun	℞	1/73	
Sunbeam	℞	7/70	
Viper	℞	1/68	①
Wolf	℞	6/73	
Yataghan	℞	2/71	
Zebra	℞	6/71	

① *Rebuilt from A11 type*
② *Fire Ball and Fire King rebuilt from Priam class A13*

Snake (A24) was built originally as a tender locomotive by the Haigh Foundry and delivered on 7 September 1838. It was renamed Exe in 1846 for working on the South Devon Railway and may have been rebuilt as a tank locomotive at this time although details are uncertain. As seen here, the 2-2-2ST is shunting at Oxford with its original name restored. Our photograph, a fortunate find in the Bodlean library, must illustrate the numerous rebuilt saddle tanks of several early types which took place in the period 1846-1850, which later became the Wolf class. Snake ceased work in November 1869.

A25	Wolf class	2-2-2T

TOTAL: 3   PERIOD: 1846-72
BUILDER: Rebuilt from 2-2-2, see A11
CYLINDERS: 15in x 18in
DRIVING WHEELS: 7ft 0in
CARRYING WHEELS: 4ft 0in

NAME	NEW	WDN
Aeolus	®	4/67
Apollo	®	8/67
Vulcan	®	4/68

A31	Leo class	2-4-0

TOTAL: 18   PERIOD: 1841-?
BUILDER: Fenton, Murray & Jackson (FMJ), R & W Hawthorn & Co (Haw), Rothwell & Co (Roth)
CYLINDERS: 15in x 18in
DRIVING WHEELS: 5ft 0in
CARRYING WHEELS: 3ft 6in

NAME	NEW	WDN	BUILDER	Leo	10/41	®	Roth
Elephant	1/41	®	Haw	Virgo	12/41	®	Roth
Buffalo	3/41	®	Haw	Libra	2/42	®	Roth
Dromedary	3/41	®	Haw	Scorpio	2/42	®	Roth
Hecla	4/41	®	FMJ	Capricornus	4/42	®	Roth
Stromboli	4/41	®	FMJ	Sagittarius	4/42	®	Roth
Etna	6/41	®	FMJ	Aquarius	6/42	®	Roth
Aries	6/41	®	Roth	Pisces	7/42	®	Roth
Taurus	7/41	®	Roth				
Gemini	9/41	®	Roth	® All rebuilt as 2-4-0T, see A41			
Cancer	10/41	®	Roth				

Vulcan (A25), built originally with a tender by Tayleur at the Vulcan Foundry, Newton-le-Willows, was one of the first locomotives delivered to the railway and the first to tried in steam, on 28 December 1837 near Iver. One of the slightly more successful of the early locomotives, it was nonetheless one of several locomotives rebuilt as a 2-2-2T back tank from 1846.

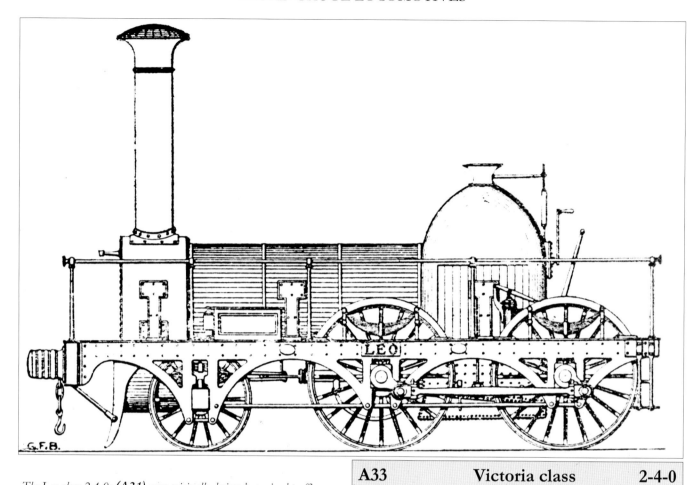

The Leo class 2-4-0s (A31) were originally designed as mixed traffic locomotives. They proved to be too light but found useful employment on the South Devon and Weymouth lines where they were recorded on the first trains to Laira, Torquay and Warminster. All were rebuilt as saddle tanks, probably between 1846 and 1850.

A32	Abbot class	4-4-0

TOTAL: 10   PERIOD: 1855-76
BUILDER: R Stephenson & Co Ltd.
CYLINDERS: 17in x 24in
DRIVING WHEELS: 7ft 0in
CARRYING WHEELS: 4ft 3in

NAME	NEW	WDN
Lalla Rookh	2/55	12/72
Ivanhoe	3/55	9/76
Robin Hood	3/55	11/76
Rob Roy	4/55	2/72
Waverley	4/55	6/76
Couer de Lion	5/55	6/76
Pirate	5/55	6/76
Abbot	6/55	10/76
Red Gauntlet	6/55	11/76

A33	Victoria class	2-4-0

TOTAL: 18   PERIOD: 1856-80

BUILDER: Great Western Railway
CYLINDERS: 16in x 24in
DRIVING WHEELS: 6ft 6in
CARRYING WHEELS: 4ft 0in

NAME	NEW	WDN
Napoleon	8/56	8/80
Victoria	8/56	1/79
Leopold	9/56	1/76
Oscar	9/56	8/80
Abdul Medjid	10/56	12/77
Victor Emanuel	10/56	6/78
Alexander	11/56	3/78
Otho	11/56	9/80
Brunel	5/63	3/79
Locke	5/63	6/81
Stephenson	6/63	12/78
Trevithick	7/63	12/78
Smeaton	8/63	2/77
Fulton	1/64	11/76
Watt	2/64	2/80
Telford	4/64	2/79
Rennie	4/64	12/78
Brindley	5/64	3/79

*The 10 Abbot class 4-4-0s **(A32)** were built by Robert Stephenson & Co in Newcastle in 1855. These were the only 4-4-0 tender locomotives to work on the broad gauge; they found extensive use in South Wales and on the Wilts, Somerset & Weymouth line. This one, Rob Roy, was an early withdrawal in February 1872 and all had gone by the end of 1876. It is coupled to a tender that features both a porter's seat, from which a porter could keep an eye on the train, and a warning gong that would be connected to the train's communication cord.*

*The Victoria class **(A33)**, 18 2-4-0 locomotives built at Swindon from August 1856, were generally useful locomotives and were particularly associated with the Weymouth line. On 26 August 1862 the last down train due at Weymouth at 10pm, hauled by Victoria, ran out of control whilst descending Upwey bank. It crashed through the station and only just stopped short of the adjacent Somerset Hotel, thereby giving rise to a song whose chorus refers to "Victoria in the gin shop!" The first eight were named after European heads of state, however an additional ten locomotives, including Rennie seen here, were named after famous engineers. All had been withdrawn by mid 1881.*

A34	Metropolitan class		2-4-0

TOTAL: 7   PERIOD: C.1865-73
BUILDER: Rebuilt from 2-4-0T, see A43
CYLINDERS: 16in x 24in
DRIVING WHEELS: 6ft 0in
CARRYING WHEELS: 3ft 6in

NAME	NEW	WDN
Hornet	®	6/73
Mogul	®	6/72
Azalia	®	6/72
Lily	®	12/72
Myrtle	®	12/73
Violet	®	6/72
Laurel	®	6/72

A35	Hawthorn class		2-4-0

TOTAL: 26   PERIOD: 1865-92
BUILDER: Stothert, Slaughter & Co (③   Great Western Railway)
CYLINDERS: 16in x 24in
DRIVING WHEELS: 6ft 0in
CARRYING WHEELS: 4ft 0in

NAME	NEW	WDN
Hawthorn	4/65	3/76
Hackworth	5/65	5/92
John Gray	5/65	3/76
Murdock	5/65	5/92

Melling	5/65	® 1877	
Gooch	5/65	5/92	
Hedley	6/65	® 1877	
Roberts	6/65	® 1877	
Bury	7/65	® 1877	
Fenton	7/65	5/92	
Dewrance	7/65	5/92	
Foster	9/65	9/76	
Blenkensop	12/65	5/92	
Avonside	12/65	1/92	①
Beyer	12/65	® 1877	
Hawk	12/65	5/92	②
Ostrich	12/65	® 1877	②
Penn	1/66	® 1877	
Peacock	1/66	6/76	
Stewart	1/66	® 1877	
Phlegethon	1/66	1/87	②
Pollux	2/66	® 1877	②
Sharp	2/66	2/87	③
Wood	2/66	5/92	
Acheron	2/66	2/87	②③
Cerebus	2/66	® 1877	②

® *Ten locomotives were rebuilt as 2-4-0ST, see A44.*
① *Avonside was delivered with the name **Slaughter** but renamed soon after delivery to reflect the change in name of its builders from Stothert, Slaughter & Co to the Avonside Engine Co.*
② *Built by the Great Western Railway.*
③ *Sharp in 1/86 and Acheron in 6/86 were taken out of service for rebuilding but both were condemned in 2/87 without returning to service*

2-4-0 Pollux (A35) was built at Swindon in February 1866, one of the last of the Hawthorn class of 26 locomotives, twenty of which had been built by Stothert, Slaughter & Co in Bristol. Pollux is seen here at Swindon when newly delivered, exhibiting the scafed pea green lining style but attached to an older tender which is lined in the thick straw colour. The names continued the engineers' theme from the Victoria class, however this one was officially a renewal so carried a classical name transferred from a Priam class 2-2-2 (A13).

Hawthorn class 2-4-0 Hawk (A35) was again built at Swindon, this time in December 1865 but shown in later condition prior to withdrawal. In their last years they were used extensively as station pilots at Swindon, Bristol, Taunton, and Newton Abbot. Hawk is seen outside Bath Road shed at Bristol and carries a tender weather board and mixed gauge buffers.

A36		2-4-0

TOTAL: 1   PERIOD: 1886-92
BUILDER: Great Western Railway
CYLINDERS: 14in x 21in + 22in x 21in compound
DRIVING WHEELS: 7ft 0½in
CARRYING WHEELS: 4ft 0½in

NUMBER	NEW	WDN
8	6/86	5/92

A37		2-4-0

TOTAL: 2   PERIOD: 1888-92
BUILDER: Great Western Railway
CYLINDERS: 20in x 24in
DRIVING WHEELS: 7ft 0½in
CARRYING WHEELS: 4ft 6½in (originally 4ft 0½in)

NUMBER	NEW	WDN
14	5/88	5/92
16	6/88	5/92

In 1888 Dean produced two handsome express passenger 2-4-0s (A37) particularly for working the very heavy 3pm up express from Bristol to Swindon, where locomotives were changed. As built number 14, and probably its sister number 16, came out with straight running plates at the leading end with 4ft 0½in carrying wheels. Details of the date when number 14 was rebuilt into the form seen in the photograph are lacking but it was presumably in about 1890. When withdrawn these two locomotives were laid aside for conversion to standard gauge, however this was not undertaken and they were cut up in 1894.

A38	3501 class	2-4-0

TOTAL: 5   PERIOD: 1890-92
BUILDER: Rebuilt from 2-4-0T, see A45
CYLINDERS: 17in x 26in
DRIVING WHEELS: 5ft 1in
CARRYING WHEELS: 3ft 6in

NUMBER	NEW	WDN	
3501	11/90	© 5/92	
3502	5/90	© 5/92	①
3505	5/90	© 5/92	
3507	5/90	© 5/92	
3508	5/91	© 5/92	

① *3502 ceased running on the broad gauge before the gauge conversion weekend*

3501 class 2-4-0 3508 **(A38)** *was originally built as a 2-4-0T, but together with 3502 and 3505 were converted to tender locomotives in May 1890 for working the newly introduced Cornishman express non-stop between Exeter and Plymouth. Subsequently two more were so treated and the remaining tank locomotives were rebuilt with tenders on conversion to the narrow gauge.*

A41	Leo class	2-4-0ST

TOTAL: 18   PERIOD: ?-1874
BUILDER: Rebuilt from 2-4-0, see A31.
CYLINDERS: 15in x 18in
DRIVING WHEELS: 5ft 0in
CARRYING WHEELS: 3ft 6in

NAME	NEW	WDN
Elephant	®	9/70
Buffalo	®	4/65
Dromedary	®	12/63
Hecla	®	9/64
Stromboli	®	11/69
Etna	®	12/70
Aries	®	6/71
Taurus	®	12/70
Gemini	®	3/66
Cancer	®	6/74
Leo	®	9/70
Virgo	®	8/70
Libra	®	3/71
Scorpio	®	9/72
Capricornus	®	12/69
Sagittarius	®	6/71
Aquarius	®	7/70
Pisces	®	6/74

*Leo class 2-4-0ST Aries **(A41)** is seen outside Farringdon shed in 1868. In common with the other Leo class locomotives it was rebuilt from a tender locomotive circa 1850. As tank locomotives they were used extensively on the branch lines east of Swindon and on the West London line. All were withdrawn by 1874, however Aries had ceased to work in 1871.*

A42	Bogie class		4-4-0ST

Horace	9/54	10/80			
Virgil	9/54	12/73			
Ovid	10/54	3/72			
Juvenal	11/54	12/73			
Seneca	11/54	3/72			
Lucretius	12/54	3/72			
Theocritus	12/54	12/73			
Statius	1/55	10/71			
Euripides	2/55	12/71			
Hesiod	3/55	6/72			
Lucan	3/55	3/72			

TOTAL: 13   PERIOD: 1849-80
BUILDER: R & W Hawthorn & Co (① Great Western Railway)
CYLINDERS: 17in x 24in
DRIVING WHEELS: 5ft 9in (① 6ft 0in)
CARRYING WHEELS: 3ft 6in

NAME	NEW	WDN	
Corsair	8/49	6/73	①
Brigand	9/49	6/73	①
Sappho	6/54	12/73	
Homer	8/54	12/73	

① *Corsair and Brigand were built by the Great Western Railway. They had 7ft 0in driving wheels*

*The 4-4-0ST Bogie class **(A42)** were built by Hawthorn & Co from 1854 as a development of Gooch's Corsair and Brigand of 1849. The first pair had been used in South Devon but the purpose of building this second batch is something of a mystery. We know that some were used on short-distance secondary traffic such as between Gloucester and Hereford, and others were used as shunting locomotives. After the amalgamation with the SDR in 1876 this locomotive, Horace, was sent down to South Devon and was withdrawn in 1880*

A43 Metropolitan class 2-4-0T

TOTAL: 22 PERIOD: 1862-77
BUILDER: Great Western Railway (GWR), Kitson & Co (Kit),
          Vulcan Foundry (VF)
CYLINDERS: 16in x 24in
DRIVING WHEELS: 6ft 0in
CARRYING WHEELS: 3ft 6in

NAME	BUILDER	NEW	WDN
Hornet	VF	6/62	®
Shah	Kit	6/62	6/72
Bee	VF	7/62	12/74
Gnat	VF	7/62	6/74
Bey	Kit	7/62	6/72
Wasp	VF	8/62	6/77
Mosquito	VF	8/62	12/74
Locust	VF	8/62	12/76
Czar	Kit	8/62	6/71
Mogul	Kit	8/62	®
Kaiser	Kit	9/62	6/72
Khan	Kit	9/62	12/72
Rose	GWR	8/63	10/77
Thistle	GWR	9/63	6/74
Fleur de Lis	GWR	11/63	12/72
Shamrock	GWR	11/63	10/77
Camelia	GWR	12/63	6/76
Azalia	GWR	4/64	®
Lily	GWR	5/64	®
Myrtle	GWR	5/64	®
Violet	GWR	7/64	®
Laurel	GWR	10/64	®

® *Seven locomotives were rebuilt c.1865 as 2-4-0s, see A34.*

*Ostrich, one of ten Hawthorns rebuilt as 2-4-0STs in 1877 (**A44**) which were then used extensively in the South West. It is seen newly outshopped from Newton Abbot works in 1890.*

A44	Hawthorn class	2-4-0T

TOTAL: 10   PERIOD: 1877-92
BUILDER: Rebuilt from 2-4-0, see A35.
CYLINDERS: 17in x 24in
DRIVING WHEELS: 5ft 0in
CARRYING WHEELS: 4ft 0in

NAME	NEW	WDN
Melling	Ⓡ 1877	5/92
Hedley	Ⓡ 1877	5/92
Roberts	Ⓡ 1877	5/92
Bury	Ⓡ 1877	5/92
Beyer	Ⓡ 1877	1/87
Ostrich	Ⓡ 1877	5/92
Penn	Ⓡ 1877	5/92
Stewart	Ⓡ 1877	5/92
Pollux	Ⓡ 1877	5/92
Cerebus	Ⓡ 1877	5/92

A45	3501 class	2-4-0T

TOTAL: 10   PERIOD: 1885-92
BUILDER: Great Western Railway
CYLINDERS: 17in x 26in
DRIVING WHEELS: 5ft 1in
CARRYING WHEELS: 3ft 6in

NUMBER	NEW	WDN	
3501	3/85	Ⓡ 11/90	
3502	4/85	Ⓡ 5/90	
3503	4/85	Ⓒ 5/92	
3504	5/85	Ⓒ 5/92	
3505	5/85	Ⓡ 5/90	
3506	6/85	Ⓒ 5/92	①
3507	6/85	Ⓡ 5/91	
3508	6/85	Ⓡ 5/90	
3509	6/85	Ⓒ 5/92	
3510	6/85	Ⓒ 5/92	

Ⓡ   *Five locomotives rebuilt as 2-4-0, see A38.*
①   *3506 ceased running on the broad gauge before the gauge conversion weekend.*

*The 3501 class convertible 2-4-0Ts **(A45)** were intended for working over the South Devon banks west of Newton Abbot. Whilst intended for express passenger use, they could also be found on lesser duties. Half the class were rebuilt as tender locomotives (A38) but 3504 remained as a tank locomotive until converted to narrow gauge in June 1892.*

A46	3521 class	0-4-2ST

TOTAL: 19   PERIOD: 1888-91
BUILDER: Great Western Railway
CYLINDERS: 17in x 24in
DRIVING WHEELS: 5ft 0in
CARRYING WHEELS: 4ft 0in

NUMBER	NEW	WDN
3541	9/88	® 4/90
3542	9/88	® 1/91
3543	9/88	© 9/91
3544	10/88	® 5/90
3545	10/88	® 4/91
3546	10/88	® 8/90
3547	10/88	© 6/91
3548	11/88	® 1/91
3549	11/88	® 4/91
3550	11/88	® 9/90
3551	11/88	® 7/90
3552	12/88	® 10/90
3553	12/88	® 5/90
3554	1/89	® 3/91
3555	1/89	® 11/90
3556	2/89	® 8/90
3557	3/89	® 2/91
3558	6/89	® 9/90
3559	7/89	® 10/90

® *17 locomotives rebuilt as 0-4-4Ts; 3560 was built as an 0-4-4T, see A47.*

A47	3521 class	0-4-4T

TOTAL: 18   PERIOD: 1889-92
BUILDER: Great Western Railway
CYLINDERS: 17in x 24in
DRIVING WHEELS: 5ft 0in
CARRYING WHEELS: 3ft 6in

NUMBER	NEW	WDN
3541	® 4/90	© 2/92
3542	® 1/91	© 5/92
3544	® 5/90	© 5/92
3545	® 4/91	© 5/92
3546	® 8/90	© 5/92
3548	® 1/91	© 5/92
3549	® 4/91	© 5/92
3550	® 9/90	© 5/92
3551	® 7/90	© 4/92
3552	® 10/90	© 5/92
3553	® 5/90	© 5/92
3554	® 3/91	© 2/92
3555	® 11/90	© 5/92
3556	® 8/90	© 4/92
3557	® 2/91	© 5/92
3558	® 9/90	© 5/92
3559	® 10/90	© 5/92
3560	7/89	© 5/92

® *All except 3560 were rebuilt from 0-4-2STs, see A46.*

*3547 was a 3521 class convertible 0-4-2ST (**A46**) built at Swindon in October 1888. It was one of a complex class of locomotives that proved themselves unsteady at speed, so much so that the last one was produced as an 0-4-4T with side and well tanks. 3547 was rebuilt in this form in 1891 at which time it was converted to narrow gauge (as was 3542) so ran as a broad gauge locomotive for less than three years, however all the remaining saddle tanks were converted to broad gauge 0-4-4Ts (**A47**).*

3560 (A47) was built at Swindon in July 1889, the first of the 3521 class to be built as a side tank. All the earlier 0-4-2STs were rebuilt in this form but even then they were still unsteady at speed. Following conversion to narrow gauge, several were involved in serious accidents and so all were completely rebuilt in the late 1890s as tender locomotives.

A51	Fury class	0-6-0

TOTAL: 4   PERIOD: 1842-71
BUILDER: Nasmyth, Gaskell & Co
CYLINDERS: 15in x 18in
DRIVING WHEELS: 5ft 0in

NAME	NEW	WDN
Hercules	7/42	7/70
Sampson	7/42	7/70
Goliah	8/42	3/71
Tityos	10/42	7/70

A52		0-6-0

TOTAL: 1   PERIOD: 1846-?
BUILDER: Stothert & Slaughter
CYLINDERS: 17in x 24in
DRIVING WHEELS: 5ft 0in

NAME	NEW	WDN
Avalanche	2/46	®

® *Rebuilt as 0-6-0ST, see A61.*

A53	Fury class	0-6-0

TOTAL: 12   PERIOD: 1846-72
BUILDER: Great Western Railway
CYLINDERS: 16in x 24in
DRIVING WHEELS: 5ft 0in or 4ft 6in

NAME	NEW	WDN	WHEELS
Premier	2/46	11/69	5ft 0in?
Ajax	5/46	8/71	5ft 0in?
Argo	7/46	3/66	4ft 6in
Bellerophon	7/46	4/70	5ft 0in?
Vesuvius	9/46	4/70	4ft 6in
Dreadnought	10/46	4/71	5ft 0in?
Telica	11/46	7/70	4ft 6in
Fury	12/46	2/71	5ft 0in?
Bergion	1/47	11/70	5ft 0in
Briareus	2/47	12/70	5ft 0in?
Brontes	5/47	6/72	5ft 0in?
Jason	5/47	9/70	5ft 0in?

*In February 1846 Fury class 0-6-0 **(A53)** Premier was the first locomotive erected at Swindon, though its boiler was supplied by a contractor, probably R Stephenson & Co. In many ways she was the prototype of a large series of 0-6-0 goods locomotives though these were the last to be built with a haycock firebox. It was cut up in November 1869.*

A54	Caesar class	0-6-0

TOTAL: 6   PERIOD: 1847-73
BUILDER: Great Western Railway
CYLINDERS: 16in x 24in
DRIVING WHEELS: 5ft 0in

NAME	NEW	WDN
Pyracmon	11/47	3/72
Steropes	1/48	8/71
Caliban	2/48	4/73
Behemoth	3/48	12/73
Mammoth	4/48	7/72
Alligator	7/48	12/73

A55	Fury class	0-6-0

TOTAL: 1   PERIOD: 1849-69
BUILDER: Great Western Railway
CYLINDERS: 16in x 24in
DRIVING WHEELS: 5ft 0in

NAME	NEW	WDN	
Bacchus	5/49	11/69	①

① *Built using parts from Hurricane (A02).*

A56	Caeser class	0-6-0

TOTAL: 8   PERIOD: 1851-80
BUILDER: Great Western Railway
CYLINDERS: 17in x 24in (initially 16in x 24in)
DRIVING WHEELS: 5ft 0in

NAME	NEW	WDN
Dido	6/51	11/72
Volcano	6/51	6/74
Thunderer	7/51	6/74
Caesar	8/51	3/80
Florence	11/51	6/74
Nora Creina	11/51	5/72
Hero	12/51	6/71
Druid	2/52	3/79

*Caesar class 0-6-0 Dido **(A56)** was built in June 1851, the first of eight similar locomotives. These were the immediate successors of the Pyracmon series (A54) of 1847 from which they differed in only small details, and were the immediate predecessors of the larger Gooch standard 0-6-0s (A57). Dido ceased work in November 1872 but Caesar was not cut up until March 1880 and so outlived many of the later standard locomotives.*

A57   Caeser class   0-6-0

TOTAL: 102   PERIOD: 1852-92
BUILDER: Great Western Railway
CYLINDERS: 17in x 24in
DRIVING WHEELS: 5ft 0in

NAME	NEW	WDN
Flirt	5/52	3/74
Giaour	5/52	11/76
Hebe	5/52	7/77
Pearl	5/52	2/78
Ariadne	11/52	6/79
Leander	12/52	6/75
Cato	3/53	6/71
Europa	3/53	5/92
Nelson	4/53	10/73
Trafalgar	6/53	1/71
Cicero	7/53	1/71
Ulysses	7/53	12/72
Diana	8/53	10/77
Minerva	8/53	10/77
Cupid	10/53	11/74
Coquette	10/53	12/75
Psyche	10/53	6/74
Hecuba	11/53	6/73
Romulus	11/53	10/77
Remus	11/53	5/79
Wellington	11/53	12/73
Monarch	12/53	12/79
Zina	12/53	6/74
Brutus	1/54	6/74

NAME	NEW	WDN
Ceres	1/54	10/77
Ruby	1/54	6/81
Flora	2/54	12/72
Thames	2/54	10/77
Neptune	3/54	8/81
Vesper	3/54	3/79
Iris	3/54	3/74
Cyprus	4/54	12/78
Caliph	5/54	12/78
Janus	5/54	10/80
Orson	6/54	6/74
Vixen	6/54	5/79
Sibyl	8/54	12/78
Salus	8/54	3/77
Banshee	9/54	12/79
Sphinx	9/54	12/73
Cambyses	11/54	10/77
Midas	11/54	4/75
Nimrod	11/54	10/77
Geryon	12/54	11/76
Nero	1/55	10/77
Nemesis	1/55	10/77
Octavia	2/55	12/73
Plutus	2/55	3/74
Zetes	2/55	10/77
Metis	3/55	10/77
Rhea	4/55	6/72
Typhon	4/55	12/79
Osiris	5/55	10/77
Pelops	5/55	3/76
Creon	3/56	5/72

Panthea	3/56	11/78		Lagoon	3/61	5/76
Amphion	4/56	10/77		Talbot	3/61	10/77
Magi	5/56	12/79		Warhawk	3/61	6/77
Pallas	5/56	2/79		Warrior	3/61	12/72
Gyfeillon	6/56	8/79		Severus	6/61	11/78
Mersey	1/57	7/79		Sirius	6/61	10/80
Severn	2/57	12/73		Pioneer	7/61	6/77
Tweed	2/57	11/74		Hades	8/61	11/78
Avon	6/57	3/77		Chronus	9/61	12/78
Esk	6/57	7/80		Orpheus	9/61	10/77
Humber	6/57	12/83		Olympus	10/61	9/79
Boyne	8/57	3/74		Plutarch	9/62	8/75
Liffey	8/57	3/72		Regulus	10/62	6/83
Shannon	8/57	1/80		Cossack	10/62	6/80
Clyde	8/58	1/71		Tantalus	11/62	6/76
Forth	8/58	2/78		Theseus	11/62	10/80
Tay	9/58	3/81		Champion	12/62	3/78
Wear	4/59	12/79		Sylla	12/62	2/79
Tyne	5/59	4/77		Leonidas	1/63	6/81
Wye	5/59	12/79		Pandora	1/63	2/80
Plym	6/59	4/75		Xerxes	1/63	12/82
Rhondda	6/59	8/77		Luna	2/63	11/80
Tamar	6/59	1/80		Ethon	3/63	12/83
Gladiator	3/61	10/77				

Europa (A57) was the only one of these locomotives to survive to the end of the broad gauge. It was renewed at Swindon in June 1869 with a new boiler. Subsequently rebuilt with a new smokebox, chimney and cab, it latterly worked from Plymouth where it is seen.

Caesar class 0-6-0 Zetes (A57), one of Gooch's standard goods series, is seen here as running circa 1870 in beautiful condition at Gloucester Horton Road shed with the old Gloucester workhouse in the background. There were 102 locomotives in this series built over 13 years; this one was built at Swindon in February 1855 and withdrawn in October 1877.

Ethon (A57) was built at Swindon in March 1863 and seen here in final condition at Westbourne Park circa 1880. By this time the remaining Caesars had acquired Armstrong roll-top chimneys as seen here.

A58				Swindon class			0-6-0

TOTAL: 14   PERIOD: 1865-92
BUILDER: Great Western Railway
CYLINDERS: 17in x 24in
DRIVING WHEELS: 5ft 0in

NAME	NEW	WDN	TO BER	NO.	GWR NO.	WDN	
Swindon	11/65	6/74	9/74	**109**	2090	11/88	
London	12/65	6/73	6/73	**100**	2081	10/88	
Bristol	12/65	6/73	7/73	**101**	2082	10/88	
Bath	1/66	1874	3/74	**105**	2086	6/88	
Windsor	1/66	1873	4/73	**99**	2080	1/89	
Oxford	2/66	6/74	7/74	**108**	2089	12/89	
Reading	2/66	1874	5/74	**107**	2088	5/92	
Birmingham	2/66	6/73	8/73	**103**	2084	6/89	
Wolverhampton	2/66	1874	2/74	**104**	2085	12/89	
Chester	3/66	1873	4/73	**98**	2079	4/87	
Gloucester	3/66	6/73	7/73	**102**	2083	12/91	
Hereford	3/66	6/72	7/72	**97**	2078	10/88	
Newport	3/66	1874	5/74	**106**	2087	6/89	
Shrewsbury	3/66	6/72	7/72	**96**	2077	2/87	①

All these locomotives were sold to the Bristol & Exeter Railway when they lost their names in exchange for numbers. On return to the GWR in 1876 they were given new numbers but did not regain their names.

①   2077 was taken out of service 3/86 for rebuilding but was condemned 2/87 without returning to service.

*Above - 388 class 0-6-0 1204 **(A59)** was photographed outside Bristol Bath Road shed sometime after reboilering in July 1890. It was one of twenty Armstrong narrow gauge goods locomotives that were converted between February 1884 and June 1888 to run on the broad gauge, thus permitting the withdrawal of many of the older tender goods locomotives. They were used largely on mineral traffic west of Exeter and sometimes on the overnight perishable trains between the south west and London. They were all converted back to narrow gauge between March and December 1892.*

*Opposite - A Swindon class 0-6-0 **(A58)** built at Swindon as Oxford in February 1866. These 14 locomotives were essentially enlarged Caesars but unfortunately there is no known photograph of them in original condition. They were progressively sold to the B&ER between 1872 and 1874, only to be reacquired by the GWR on amalgamation in 1876. The B&ER removed their names and numbered them, with Oxford becoming number 108. In 1876 it then became GWR 2089 and was withdrawn in December 1889. Only 2088 (old Reading) survived until May 1892.*

A59	388 class	0-6-0

TOTAL: 20   PERIOD: 1884-92
BUILDER: Great Western Railway
CYLINDERS: 17in x 24in
DRIVING WHEELS: 5ft 0in

NUMBER	NEW	WDN
1196	© 6/88	© 5/92
1197	© 7/87	© 5/92
1198	© 8/88	© 5/92
1199	© 12/87	© 5/92
1200	© 2/87	© 5/92
1201	© 6/88	© 5/92
1202	© 10/87	© 3/92 ①
1203	© 6/87	© 5/92
1204	© 5/88	© 5/92
1205	© 4/88	© 5/92
1206	© 2/84	© 5/92
1207	© 5/84	© 5/92 ①
1208	© 5/84	© 5/92
1209	© 3/84	© 5/92
1210	© 2/84	© 5/92
1211	© 4/84	© 5/92
1212	© 5/84	© 5/92
1213	© 2/84	© 5/92
1214	© 9/84	© 5/92
1215	© 4/84	© 5/92

① 1202 and 1207 ceased running on the broad gauge before the gauge conversion weekend

A61	Banking class	0-6-0

TOTAL: 5   PERIOD: 1852-89
BUILDER: Great Western Railway
CYLINDERS: 17in x 24in
DRIVING WHEELS: 5ft 0in

NAME	NEW	WDN
Avalanche	®	8/65
Juno	10/52	2/89 ①
Iago	10/52	7/81
Plato	9/54	12/83
Bithon	10/54	6/71

® Avalanche was rebuilt from an 0-6-0, see A52.

*① Juno was withdrawn 6/72 and sold to the South Devon Railway in 9/72 where it was renamed **Stromboli**. On returning to the Great Western Railway in 1876 it retained its new name and was additionally given the number **2138**.*

A62   Sir Watkin class   0-6-0

TOTAL: 6   PERIOD: 1866-?
BUILDER: Great Western Railway
CYLINDERS: 17in x 24in
DRIVING WHEELS: 4ft 6in

NAME	NEW	WDN	SOLD	1876 No.	WDN
Miles	9/66				®
Bulkeley	10/66	6/72	8/72	**2157**	® ①
Sir Watkin	10/66				®
Whetham	11/66				®
Saunders	11/66	2/72	2/72	**2159**	® ①
Fowler	11/66	6/72	7/72	**2158**	® ①

®   *All six locomotives were rebuilt as 0-6-0STs in 1883 or later, see A63.*
①   *Saunders was sold to the South Devon Railway and Bulkeley and Fowler were sold to the Cornwall Railway. They were fitted with a small saddle tank above the side tanks.*

A63   Sir Watkin class   0-6-0

TOTAL: 6   PERIOD: 1880s-92
BUILDER: Rebuilt, from 0-6-0Ts, see A62.
CYLINDERS: 17in x 24in
DRIVING WHEELS: 4ft 6in (1 5ft 0in)

NAME		NEW	WDN	
Miles		®	6/88	
Bulkeley	2157	®	12/90	①
Sir Watkin		®	5/92	
Whetham		®	6/89	②
Saunders	2159	®	5/92	①
Fowler	2158	®	4/87	①③

®   *All locomotives were rebuilt not earlier than 1883.*
①   *Bulkeley, Fowler and Saunders carried numbers in addition to names as they had been operated by the South Devon and Cornwall railways.*
②   *Whetham had 5ft 0in driving wheels.*
③   *Fowler taken out of service for rebuilding in 8/86 but was condemned in 4/87 without returning to service.*

Opposite - The Sir Watkin tanks (A63) were built with 1,015 gallon tanks. Photographs of those working on the CR and SDR show an additional small tank fitted above the boiler and behind the dome, but they were recorded as having just 750 gallon capacity in 1876 and 1883. After this all six were fitted with 1,030 gallon saddle tanks. This photograph shows Miles again, now with its saddle tank, shunting at Taunton in 1885. It ceased work in June 1888.

Sir Watkin class 0-6-0ST (A62) Miles was built at Swindon in September 1866. It was one of six locomotives built with condensing apparatus for use on the Metropolitan Railway, but this was removed in 1869. Two were sold to the Cornwall Railway and another to the South Devon Railway, but all six were reunited on the GWR in 1876.

A64	1076 class	0-6-0ST

TOTAL: 50   PERIOD: 1876-92
BUILDER: Great Western Railway
CYLINDERS: 17in x 24in
DRIVING WHEELS: 4ft 6in

NUMBER	NEW	WDN		NUMBER	NEW	WDN
1228	10/76	© 5/92		1248	© 12/87	© 5/92
1229	10/76	© 5/92		1249	© 8/87	© 5/92
1230	11/76	© 5/92		1250	© 11/88	© 5/92
1231	11/76	© 5/92		1251	© 6/88	© 5/92
1232	11/76	© 5/92		1252	© 7/88	© 5/92
1233	11/76	© 5/92		1253	© 7/87	© 5/92
1234	11/76	© 5/92		1254	© 7/87	© 5/92
1235	12/76	© 5/92 ①		1255	© 6/87	© 5/92
1236	12/76	© 5/92		1256	© 6/87	© 5/92
1237	12/76	© 5/92		1257	© 6/87	© 5/92
1238	© 12/88	© 5/92		1561	11/78	© 5/92
1239	© 7/87	© 5/92		1562	11/78	© 5/92
1240	© 12/88	© 5/92		1563	12/78	© 5/92
1241	© 12/87	© 10/91		1564	12/78	© 5/92
1242	© 5/87	© 5/92		1565	12/78	© 5/92
1243	© 9/88	© 5/92		1566	© 5/84	© 5/92
1244	© 6/88	© 5/92		1567	© 12/84	© 5/92
1245	© 9/88	© 5/92		1568	© 8/84	© 5/92
1246	© 10/87	© 5/92		1569	© 12/84	© 5/92
1247	© 2/87	© 5/92		1570	© 3/84	© 5/92
				1571	© 8/84	© 5/92
				1572	© 9/84	© 5/92
				1573	© 8/84	© 5/92
				1574	© 11/84	© 5/92
				1575	© 11/84	© 5/92

1576	© 7/84	© 5/92
1577	© 8/84	© 5/92 ②
1578	© 6/84	© 5/92 ②
1579	© 5/84	© 5/92 ②
1580	© 5/84	© 5/92 ②

① *1235 ceased running on the broad gauge before the gauge conversion weekend.*

② *1577-1580 were charged to the Cornwall Railway from 12/84.*

A91	Replica locomotives		2-2-2

TOTAL: 3

NAME	BUILDER	NEW	
North Star	Great Western Railway	1925	Priam class, see A12
Iron Duke	Resco (Railways) Ltd	1985	Alma class, see A17
Fire Fly	Fire Fly Trust	2005	Priam class, see A13

Between 1876 and 1888 fifty of the narrow gauge 1076 class tank locomotives (A64) were either built or converted to run on the broad gauge. They were a large, powerful and successful class, many of which after conversion to narrow gauge, and subsequently rebuilt with pannier tanks, survived into the 1930s, some working auto trains in the Plymouth area where they had spent their broad gauge youth. 1256 was one of the last converted to the broad gauge in June 1887 and is pictured here near Plymouth shed in the last years of broad gauge working. It was converted back to narrow gauge in August 1892.

Part B - BRISTOL & EXETER RAILWAY

The Bristol & Exeter Railway was opened from Bristol to Bridgwater on 14 June 1841, and was completed to Exeter on 1 May 1844. The operation was leased to the Great Western Railway for the five years from completion and during this period it was operated as an extension of that line with the same types of locomotives as used east of Bristol.

The B&ER took on its own working from 1 May 1849 using locomotives with a distinctly Swindon parentage. Expresses were hauled by 4-2-2s (B11) that were small versions of the Alma Class (A17) then being turned out for the main line out of London, and these were joined by 0-6-0 goods locomotives (B51) similar to the Caesar Class (A54).

The next motive power was very different. A self-propelled "steam carriage" (B21) was tested for use on the branch lines. It was not very successful and was soon taken apart, although the power unit was eventually sold to a firm of contractors for powering their works trains (C84).

So far the motive power had been under the control of Charles Gregory, but James Pearson was appointed as the Locomotive Superintendent in May 1850, and under his control the railway was to build a fleet of very distinctive locomotives. His first new design was for some light 2-2-2WT locomotives (B22) for the branch lines to Clevedon and Tiverton, then in 1853 came the arrival of the first of Pearson's notable 4-2-4T locomotives (B23). The flangeless 9ft driving wheels clearly made them suitable for mainline expresses, but they were also regularly used on branch line trains.

More conventional tank locomotives in the form of 4-4-0STs (B41) followed in 1855. The next deliveries were more powerful 2-2-2WTs (B24) and a 4-2-4T (B25) in 1859, the big tank was now with smaller 7ft 6in wheels and built at the company's own workshops at Bristol. Two more 0-6-0s (B51) were added to the fleet in 1860, then another 4-2-4T and a small batch of 4-4-0STs (B42) followed in 1862. The latter now with 1,280 gallon tanks rather than the 1,100 gallon version delivered seven years earlier. Two small 0-6-0STs (B61) were built at Bristol in 1866, but the following year a large batch of 4-4-0STs (B42) were delivered from the Vulcan Foundry. Bristol then turned out a small number of 8ft 10in 4-2-4Ts (B26).

There was a pressing need for new locomotives in the 1870s. Ten 2-4-0 locomotives (B31) were built at Bristol and some narrow gauge 0-6-0s (B52) were converted to broad gauge. The whole of the relatively modern Swindon Class 0-6-0s (A58) were brought from the GWR between 1872 and 1874. For passenger trains, one last 8ft 10in 4-2-4T (B26) appeared at Bristol in 1873 and more 4-4-0STs (B43) were purchased. These now featured 1,440 gallon tanks, 30% larger than those used on the South Devon Railway. For shunting, some small 0-4-0WTs (B44) were built, some 0-6-0STs (B62) rebuilt from tender locomotives, and two locomotives bought second-hand (B63, C24). The final locomotives built at Bristol were three convertible 2-4-0s (B32).

The B&ER amalgamated with the GWR on 1 January 1876 and the locomotives were absorbed into that fleet. The 9ft 4-2-4Ts had all been withdrawn by then, but one of the 8ft 10in type derailed on 27 July 1876 and three were quickly rebuilt as more conventional 8ft 4-2-2s (B12), which left the two 7ft 6in versions to soldier on until 1880 and 1885.

Livery of the first locomotives followed the pattern set by Swindon, with brass splashers and numberplate. From about 1860 the colour was changed to a plain black and the company's initials were carried alongside the number. The B&ER was one of the few broad gauge companies that did not use names for its locomotives, and it also allocated the numbers of withdrawn locomotives to new ones. The way the numbers were moved between locomotives can be traced in the index.

B11   2-2-2

TOTAL: 20   PERIOD: 1849-89
BUILDER: Longridge & Co (RBL), Stothert & Slaughter (SS)
CYLINDERS: 16½in x 24in (① later 18in x 24in)
DRIVING WHEELS: 7ft 6in
CARRYING WHEELS: 4ft 3in

NO.	GW NO.	NEW	WDN		
1		5/49	1875	RBL	
2		5/49	1872	RBL	
3		5/49	1874	RBL	
4		5/49	1871	RBL	
5		5/49	1871	RBL	
6		5/49	1870	RBL	
7	2007	5/49	12/85	RBL	①
8		5/49	1872	RBL	
9	2008	5/49	11/89	RBL	①
10	2009	5/49	9/88	RBL	①
11		5/49	1874	SS	
12		5/49	1862	SS	
13	2010	5/49	11/78	SS	①
14		5/49	1870	SS	
15	2011	5/49	10/88	SS	①
16		5/49	1875	SS	
17	2012	5/49	12/85	SS	①
18	2013	5/49	9/80	SS	①
19	2014	5/49	12/88	SS	①
20		5/49	1874	SS	

① Rebuilt by the GWR with 18in x 24in cylinders.

B12   4-2-2

TOTAL: 3   PERIOD: 1877-90
BUILDER: Rebuilt by GWR from 4-2-4T, see B26
CYLINDERS: 18in x 24in
DRIVING WHEELS: 8ft 0in
CARRYING WHEELS: 4ft 0in + 4ft 6in

NO.	GW NO.	NEW	WDN
	2001	® 1877	12/89
	2002	® 1877	12/90
	2003	® 1877	6/84

*Most of the locomotives built for the B&ER in 1849 were 7ft 6in singles with 16½in cylinders **(B11)**, a little smaller than the Alma Class that were being built at Swindon for the GWR. Of the twenty 4-2-2s, eight such as 2009 survived to be rebuilt by the GWR with 18in cylinders.*

*All six of the 7ft 6in and 8ft 10in locomotives became GWR stock in 1876, but shortly afterwards one derailed at speed which cast some doubt on the stability of the 8ft 10in locomotives. All four were withdrawn and rebuilt as three rather more conventional 4-2-2 tender locomotives **(B12)**, such as 2001 seen here at Taunton.*

B21	Steam Carriage	0-2-4

TOTAL: 1   PERIOD: 1849-56
BUILDER: W R Adams
CYLINDERS: 8in x 12in
DRIVING WHEELS: 4ft 6in
CARRYING WHEELS: 3ft 6in

NO.	NEW	TO B&ER	SOLD
29 (Fairfield)	12/48	1/50 ®	6/56

® *Tested on West London Railway before acceptance by the Bristol & Exeter Railway. Rebuilt and sold to Hutchinson & Ritson as 0-4-0vb, see C84.*

B22		2-2-2T

TOTAL: 5   PERIOD: 1851-78
BUILDER: Longridge & Co (RBL), E. B. Wilson & Co (EBW)
CYLINDERS: 12½in x 18in
DRIVING WHEELS: 5ft 6in
CARRYING WHEELS: 3ft 6in

NO.	GW NO.	NEW	WDN	
30		1851	1875	RBL
31	2054	3/51	10/77	RBL
32	2055	5/51	6/78	EBW
33		1851	1875	EBW
34		1851	1875	EBW

The first locomotives designed by James Pearson were small 2-2-2WTs **(B22)** *for branch line work, including number 34. They had 12½in cylinders and 5ft 6in driving wheels. These locomotives' numberplates were carried on their boilers.*

B23	9ft Single	4-2-4T

TOTAL: 8   PERIOD: 1853-73
BUILDER: Rothwell & Co
CYLINDERS: 18in x 24in
DRIVING WHEELS: 9ft 0in
CARRYING WHEELS: 4ft 0in

NO.	NEW	WDN
39	12/53	c.1867
40	12/53	1873
41	12/53	1868
42	1854	1868
43	1854	1871
44	5/54	1870
45	6/54	1870
46	7/54	1870

B24		2-2-2T

TOTAL: 2   PERIOD: 1859-80
BUILDER: Rothwell & Co
CYLINDERS: 14½in x 18in
DRIVING WHEELS: 5ft 6in
CARRYING WHEELS: 3ft 6in

NO.	GW NO.	NEW	WDN
57	2056	8/59	9/77
58	2057	10/59	11/80

B25	7ft 6in Single	4-2-4T

TOTAL: 2   PERIOD: 1859-85
BUILDER: Bristol & Exeter Railway
CYLINDERS: see below
DRIVING WHEELS: 7ft 6in
CARRYING WHEELS: 4ft 0in

NO.	GW NO.	NEW	WDN	CYLINDERS
12	2005	4/62	12/85	16½in x 24in
29	2006	9/59	9/80	17in x 24in

B26	8ft 10in Single	4-2-4T

TOTAL: 4   PERIOD: 1868-77
BUILDER: Bristol & Exeter Railway
CYLINDERS: 18in x 24in
DRIVING WHEELS: 8ft 10in
CARRYING WHEELS: 4ft 0in

NO.	GW NO.	NEW	WDN
39	2001	2/68	® 7/76
40	2002	6/73	® 1877
41	2003	6/68	® 1877
42	2004	12/68	10/77

® Three rebuilt as 4-2-4, see B12.

*Above - In 1859 and 1862 two smaller singles were built at Bristol with 7ft 6in wheels. The final four, including number 42 seen here, were turned out with 8ft 10in driving wheels **(B26)**.*

*Left - Number 46 was built by Rothwell & Co in 1854 as one of James Pearson's first batch of single-driver tanks **(B23)**. The 9ft diameter driving wheel towers above the enginemen on the track. All of these locomotives were withdrawn by 1873.*

B31			2-4-0

TOTAL: 10   PERIOD: 1870-92
BUILDER: Bristol & Exeter Railway Co
CYLINDERS: 17in x 24in
DRIVING WHEELS: 6ft 7½in
CARRYING WHEELS: 4ft 0in

NO.	GW NO.	NEW	WDN
2	2015	12/72	6/88
4	2016	10/71	5/92
5	2017	12/71	5/92
6	2018	4/70	6/90
8	2019	6/72	6/89
14	2020	2/70	5/92
43	2021	6/71	5/92
44	2022	12/70	10/88
45	2023	6/70	6/88
46	2024	6/70	12/89

B32			2-4-0

TOTAL: 3   PERIOD: 1874-86
BUILDER: Bristol & Exeter Railway
CYLINDERS: 17in x 24in
DRIVING WHEELS: 6ft 4in
CARRYING WHEELS: 4ft 0in

NO.	GW NO.	NEW	WDN
11	2025	5/74	4/86
20	2026	12/74	6/86
34	2027	1/75	1/84

*2020 was one of ten 2-4-0 tender locomotives **(B31)** built at Bristol for lighter trains between 1870 and 1872. They all became GWR property and four of them survived to the end of the broad gauge operations in 1892.*

B41		4-4-0ST

TOTAL: 6   PERIOD: 1855-84
BUILDER: Rothwell & Co
CYLINDERS: 17in x 24in
DRIVING WHEELS: 5ft 6in
CARRYING WHEELS: 3ft 6in

No.	GW No.	NEW	WDN
47	2028	10/55	10/79
48	2029	12/55	6/79
49	2030	12/55	6/84
50	2031	12/55	4/84
51	2032	12/55	12/82
52	2033	1/56	7/80

Four additional locomotives were delivered by Beyer, Peacock & Co in 1862 **(B42)**. *These had slightly larger 1,280 gallon tanks. Another 10 came from the Vulcan Foundry in 1867. The photograph shows how the steps up to the cab were unusually fitted between the driving wheels.*

B42			4-4-0ST

TOTAL: 14   PERIOD: 1862-92
BUILDER: Beyer, Peacock & Co (61-64), Vulcan Foundry (65-74)
CYLINDERS: 17in x 24in
DRIVING WHEELS: 5ft 6in
CARRYING WHEELS: 3ft 6in

NO.	GW NO.	NEW	WDN
61	2034	7/62	6/84
62	2035	7/62	12/86
63	2036	7/62	7/80
64	2037	7/62	3/86
65	2038	5/66	7/80
66	2039	5/66	5/92
67	2040	5/67	6/88
68	2041	5/67	3/80
69	2042	6/67	5/92
70	2043	6/67	10/88
71	2044	7/67	12/82
72	2045	7/67	5/92
73	2046	8/67	3/89
74	2047	8/67	5/92

Opposite lower - In common with most broad gauge companies, the Bristol & Exeter found the 4-4-0ST to be a useful locomotive for branch line working. Number 52 was one of the Bristol & Exeter's first half dozen, built by Rothwell & Co in 1855 **(B41)**. *These had 1,100 gallon tanks extending the length of the boiler*

The final six 4-4-0STs were built locally by the Avonside Company in Bristol **(B43)**. *2049 is one of this batch delivered in 1872 and 1873. By deepening the tank in front of the cab the capacity could be increased to 1,440 gallons, considerably larger than the 800 gallon tanks found on some 4-4-0STs on other railways.*

B43			4-4-0ST

TOTAL: 6   PERIOD: 1872-92
BUILDER: Avonside Engine Co
CYLINDERS: 17in x 24in
DRIVING WHEELS: 5ft 6in
CARRYING WHEELS: 3ft 6in

NO.	GW No.	NEW	WDN
85	2048	11/72	5/92
86	2049	12/72	5/92
87	2050	4/73	5/92
88	2051	5/73	12/90
89	2052	7/73	5/92
90	2053	8/73	5/92

B44			0-4-0WT

TOTAL: 2   PERIOD: 1872-81
BUILDER: Bristol & Exeter Railway Co
CYLINDERS: 14in x 18in
DRIVING WHEELS: 3ft 6in

NO.	GW No.	NEW	WDN
91	2094	8/72	4/80
92	2095	10/74	2/81

B44			0-4-0WT

TOTAL: 6   PERIOD: 1874-81
BUILDER: Manning Wardle & Co
CYLINDERS: 14in x 20in
DRIVING WHEELS: 4ft 0in
CARRYING WHEELS: 3ft 6in

NO.	GW No.	NEW	WDN
110	2058	3/74	6/81 ①

① *Purchased from Brotherhood, it had previously worked on the South Wales Mineral Railway, see C24.*

*To handle goods trains when the B&ER took on its own operations in 1849, Stothert & Slaughter built eight 0-6-0s with 17in cylinders (**B51**). Four 16in versions followed in 1853, and then six more 17in locomotives by 1860. 16 survived to receive GWR numbers in 1876; 2070 had previously been B&ER 26 and has been fitted with a cab.*

B51			0-6-0

TOTAL: 18   PERIOD: 1849-87
BUILDER: Stothert & Slaughter
DRIVING WHEELS: 5ft 0in
CYLINDERS: 17in x 24in

NO.	GW NO.	NEW	WDN	
21	2065	5/49	11/84	
22	2066	5/49	12/83	
23	2067	5/49	6/85	
24	2068	5/49	12/84	
25	2069	5/49	5/84	
26	2070	5/49	5/87	
27	2071	5/49	6/83	
28	2072	5/49	11/76	
35	2073	1/53	11/76	①
36	2074	1/53	10/77	①
37	2075	2/53	12/84	①
38	2076	3/53	7/80	①
53	2059	11/56	6/85	
54		11/56	Ⓡ 9/70	
55	2061	12/56	6/84	
56		12/56	Ⓡ 1870	
59	2063	7/60	6/87	
60	2064	8/60	11/84	

Ⓡ   *54 and 56 were rebuilt as 0-6-0STs, see B62.*
①   *Locomotives built in 1853 reportedly had 16in x 24in cylinders but were shown in GWR lists as 17in.*

B52			0-6-0

TOTAL: 5   PERIOD: 1870-75
BUILDER: Worcester Engine Co
CYLINDERS: 16in
DRIVING WHEELS:
CARRYING WHEELS:

NO.	NEW	WDN
77	Ⓒ 1870	Ⓒ 1875
78	Ⓒ 1870	Ⓒ 1875
79	Ⓒ 1870	Ⓒ 1875
80	Ⓒ 1870	Ⓒ 1875
81	Ⓒ 1870	Ⓒ 1875
82	Ⓒ 1870	Ⓒ 1875

Ⓒ   *These six locomotives were built for the narrow gauge but <u>five</u> were converted to run on the broad gauge for a while. In 1876 they became GWR 1360-1365.*

B61 — 0-6-0ST

TOTAL: 2
PERIOD: 1866-90
BUILDER: Bristol & Exeter Railway
CYLINDERS: 17in x 24in
DRIVING WHEELS: 3ft 6in

No.	GW No.	New	Wdn
75	2092	3/66	3/88
76	2093	8/67	12/90

B62 — 0-6-0ST

TOTAL: 2   PERIOD: 1870-90
BUILDER: Rebuilt from 0-6-0, see B51
CYLINDERS: 17in x 24in
DRIVING WHEELS: 5ft 0in

No.	GW No.	New	Wdn
54	2060	9/70	6/88
56	2062	1870	6/90

B63 — 0-6-0T

TOTAL: 1   PERIOD: 1874-76
BUILDER: Brotherhood
CYLINDERS: 16¾in x 24in
DRIVING WHEELS: 4ft 0in

No.	GW No.	New	Wdn
111	2091	3/74	9/76

Number 2062 entered service as 0-6-0 tender locomotive number 56 in December 1856. In 1870 it was one a pair rebuilt with saddle tanks (B62), in which form it ran for 20 years.

Part C - THE SMALLER FLEETS

This section covers locomotives operated by a variety of smaller railway companies and industrial concerns. As may be imagined, surviving records are not extensive and there inevitably remain gaps in our knowledge of these locomotives. The various breakwater concerns were isolated from main line railways (at least in broad gauge days) and used a system developed by James Meadows Rendel and later continued by John Coode. These broad gauge railways were carried on timber trestles, allowing stone to be tipped between the rails to form the breakwaters.

Public railways

The **Bristol & Gloucester Railway** opened as a broad gauge line on 6 July 1844. Operation was carried out under contract by Stothert & Slaughter of Bristol. They built eleven locomotives to work the line (C31, C32, C33), most incorporating design features and possibly parts from Bury & Co. The railway was amalgamated with the narrow gauge Birmingham & Gloucester Railway to become part of the **Midland Railway** in August 1846, when all eleven locomotives passed to the MR who gave them numbers in the 2xx series. The Midland subsequently supplied six broad gauge convertibles (C37, C38) to augment the motive power on the line. All the locomotives were renumbered to the 3xx series in 1852 then further renumbered to the 4xx series in 1853. The MR introduced mixed gauge throughout by May 1854, when the convertibles were quickly converted to narrow gauge as intended and continued to run until 1873. The eight surviving former Stothert & Slaughter locomotives were offered for sale, with all being taken up by Brassey & Ogilvie for their North Devon Railway contract. Broad gauge working on the former B&GR was then restricted to a daily Bristol & Exeter Railway train serving Parkfield Colliery, which was finally abandoned in May 1872. The Midland Railway livery at the time was dark green, lined in black and white and with chrome yellow and black lettering.

The **Vale of Neath Railway** was originally a broad gauge line linking Neath with Aberdare and Merthyr Tydvil. The first section to Aberdare opened on 24 September 1851, and was briefly worked by GWR locomotives prior to the first VoNR deliveries in October 1851. Conversion to mixed gauge began in 1863, and almost all of the system had been dealt with by 1 February 1865 when the company was amalgamated with the Great Western. 19 broad and 6 narrow gauge locomotives were taken into GWR stock where they retained their VoNR numbers. The line was converted to narrow gauge in May 1872 but ex-VoNR broad gauge locomotives continued in service on other parts of the GWR until the first fortnight in October 1886.

The locomotives were typical Daniel Gooch saddle tanks, the first being 4-4-0STs (C11, C12), with 0-6-0STs appearing from 1854 (C13 - C17). The demand for these goods locomotives was such that some 4-4-0STs were rebuilt as 0-6-0STs (C15) while some 0-6-0STs were rebuilt as tender locomotives (C16) in 1860. The saddle tanks were very similar to their contemporaries on the South Devon Railway, indeed the first 0-6-0STs (C13) were built as one batch with the first 0-6-0STs for that railway (D61). VoNR locomotives were painted dark green and carried brass safety valve covers. The number was carried on a brass plate on the tank with the letters "V" and "N" either side of the locomotive number.

The **North Devon Railway & Dock Company** opened on 1 August 1854. It was operated briefly by the Bristol & Exeter Railway and then under contract by Brassey & Ogilvie from August 1855. Three 'Crewe type' locomotives (C34, C36) were built at Brassey's Canada Works in Birkenhead, followed by eight former Bristol & Gloucester locomotives obtained second-hand from the Midland Railway (C31, C32, C33). The lease was taken over by the **London & South Western Railway** on 1 January 1863 and the Brassey & Ogilvie locomotives were taken into LSWR stock. At least one other second-hand locomotive (C35) was used by Brassey & Ogilvie, and there may have been others which did not survive to be recorded by the LSWR. The line was converted to mixed gauge in 1863, although some broad gauge operation continued until 1877. During this period the LSWR used three liveries: initially Indian red with black and white lining, this was supplanted by chocolate with black, white and red lining, and finally purple brown with ochre and white lining.

The first part of the broad gauge **Carmarthen & Cardigan Railway** opened on 1 March 1860, the line eventually reaching Llandyssil on 3 June 1864, still well short of Cardigan. Worked at first by GWR locomotives, the C&CR operated its own line from 12 August 1861 with two broad gauge locomotives, which for a time was increased to four. Part of the line was altered to mixed gauge in 1866 and the whole railway was converted to narrow gauge in June 1872, following which the four broad gauge locomotives were reunited on the South Devon Railway. Two were side tanks (C21) and two were saddle tanks (C22). After rebuilding by the SDR they passed to the GWR in February 1876, and three of them survived until the end of broad gauge working in May 1892. Final amalgamation of the C&CR into the GWR took place on 1 July 1881, when three of their four narrow gauge locomotives also passed into GWR stock.

The first lines of the broad gauge **South Wales Mineral Railway** opened in June 1861. The railway was leased to and worked by the Glyncorrwg Coal Company until 1870, then by their successors the Glyncorrwg Colliery Company Ltd, using five broad gauge locomotives (C24). It was converted to narrow gauge in May 1872. One of the four remaining broad gauge locomotives was altered to narrow gauge, lasting until 1901. The others were sold to Brotherhood of Chippenham, with one passing to the Bristol & Exeter Railway and another to the Newquay & Cornwall Junction Railway. The SWMR was later taken over by the GWR on 1 January 1908 along with their five narrow gauge locomotives, which included two ex-South Devon 0-6-0STs (D65).

The **Lynvi Valley Railway** was developed from earlier 4ft 7in gauge tramways and opened as a broad gauge line on 10 August 1861. It was worked by locomotives hired from the GWR until the first of its own arrived in April 1862. The company amalgamated with the narrow gauge Ogmore Valley Railway on 1 July 1866 to form the **Lynvi & Ogmore Railway**. By 1868 the mixed gauge had been laid throughout the former LVR system, when the three broad gauge locomotives (C25, C26) were exchanged for four narrow gauge locomotives from the West Cornwall Railway. The L&OR, with twelve narrow gauge locos, was taken over by the GWR on 1 July 1873 and amalgamated on 1 July 1883. The three broad gauge locomotives, typical Gooch saddle tanks, were taken into West Cornwall stock between January and April 1868, passing to the GWR in February 1876. The last was withdrawn in June 1886. The line was converted to narrow gauge in May 1872. A picture of *Una* shows a dark (presumed green) livery with black & white lining featuring reversed corners. This is probably the builder's livery, rather than anything to do with the railway company itself. The situation was perhaps more akin to buying a traction engine, which would come in the maker's colours.

The **Metropolitan Railway** (C61) opened on 10 January 1863 as a mixed gauge line from Paddington station to Farringdon Street in London. After a brief period of GWR operation, the Metropolitan operated their own narrow gauge services over the line, whilst GWR broad gauge services ran over the route as far as Farringdon Street from 13 June 1864, to Aldersgate from 1 March 1866, and to Moorgate from 1 July 1866. Broad gauge working ceased on 1 March 1869. Before the opening of the line an experimental locomotive was tested that complied with the legal emissions requirements by utilising hot bricks to heat its steam, which is colloquially known as "Fowler's Ghost". It was not a success so Daniel Gooch introduced in 1862 a batch of 2-4-0STs with condensing gear (A43) which were supplemented by a few Armstrong 0-6-0Ts (A62) for goods traffic in 1866, although by this time the Metropolitan was working its own trains with narrow gauge 4-4-0Ts.

The broad gauge **Torbay & Brixham Railway** (C51) was opened on 28 February 1868. The South Devon Railway worked the line, but the T&BR had obtained their own well tank locomotive second-hand from Portland Breakwater. The locomotive was mortgaged to the SDR in 1870 yet continued to work the T&BR, but a new 2-4-0T then on order for the T&BR was delivered to the SDR (D47). In January 1877 the GWR sold an ex-SDR saddle tank (D52) to the T&BR. The railway was absorbed into the GWR on 1 January 1883, when the ex-SDR locomotive returned to stock but the former Portland locomotive was withdrawn. The line was converted to narrow gauge in May 1892.

The **Severn & Wye Railway & Canal Company** built up a system of 3ft 8in gauge tramways from 1813 onwards. These were generally worked by horses, but by the end of 1865 five locomotives had been obtained. On 19 April 1869 broad gauge lines were brought into use, laid alongside the 3ft 8in

over part of the system. Three of the locomotives (C27, C28) were converted to suit, and two further locomotives (C29) were delivered as broad gauge convertibles. Following the general gauge conversions in the area in May 1872 these broad gauge lines were removed and most of the 3ft 8in gauge lines converted to 4ft 8½in. The five broad gauge locomotives were converted to 4ft 8½in gauge in 1872. The railway became a Great Western/Midland joint line on 1 July 1894. Seven 4ft 8½in gauge locomotives were taken into GWR stock and six by the MR. The latter included the two former broad gauge convertibles, the last of these surviving until 1911 after further alteration.

The broad gauge **Newquay & Cornwall Junction Railway** (C52) was opened on 1 July 1869 and was worked under contract by William West & Sons of St Blazey. The 4ft 8½in **Cornwall Minerals Railway** opened on 1 July 1874 and absorbed the N&CJR on the same day, when West's locomotives were added to CMR stock. The CMR was worked by the GWR from September 1877, using 9 of the 18 former CMR narrow gauge locomotives but with the GWR's own broad gauge locomotives on the N&CJR section. The two CMR broad gauge locomotives then in use were not taken into GWR stock, instead they were sold to VJ Barton in 1879. Final amalgamation did not take place not until July 1896, when the CMR-worked Goonbarrow branch and one further narrow gauge locomotive were also taken over. The former N&CJR line remained broad gauge until May 1892.

The **Lostwithiel & Fowey Railway** was opened on 1 June 1869 and was initially operated by the Cornwall Railway but the railway took on its own operation early in 1870 (C53). The first locomotive was reported as being of insufficient power and the directors were soon looking for a larger one; in 1878 it was recorded as being worked by a locomotive belonging to Mr Treffry. Traffic on the line was suspended at the end of 1879. Work started on an extension to meet the Cornwall Minerals Railway in 1891, it being transferred to that company which reopened it as a standard gauge line in 1893.

Contractors and industrial lines

Construction work on the Harbour of Refuge at **Holyhead** commenced on 10 January 1848, and continued until 30 June 1873. The line from the quarries to the breakwater was retained for maintenance work, and remained in broad gauge use until 1913 when it was converted to narrow gauge. The contractors were J & C Rigby, who used at least eight, possibly ten, four-wheeled tank locomotives on the railway (C92). There were also about fifty mobile cranes in the quarries, some of them steam powered. With construction work nearing completion, most were sold in December 1872. One locomotive was retained for maintenance work until the line was narrowed in 1913, and was not scrapped until 1945.

Work on the gravity operated railway from the **Portland** quarries down to the Harbour of Refuge there commenced in August 1848. The first stone of the breakwater was laid by

Prince Albert on 25 July 1849, with the final stone being laid by the Prince of Wales on 10 August 1872. The breakwater was connected to the national railway system in February 1876. It was converted to narrow gauge at the same time as the main line in the area had been narrowed in June 1874. The contractor was John Towlerton Leather. He initially used horses to haul the waggons, but from 1851 steam locomotives were introduced. At least seven, possibly ten, four-wheeled tank locomotives operated on the railway (C93). With the completion of the works the four remaining locomotives passed to the Admiralty. These were sold in 1875 due to the narrowing of the railway.

Construction of **Falmouth Docks** commenced in February 1860 and development was sufficiently advanced for the Falmouth Docks & Engineering Co to receive its first ship into dry dock the following year. The Cornwall Railway reached Falmouth in August 1863 and the docks were connected to the main line by a steeply graded spur in January 1864. Three broad gauge vertical-boiler locomotives (C91) were used in the docks, the first probably in 1861, and these prompted the South Devon Railway to obtain a similar locomotive (D50) for their harbourside lines in Plymouth. One was nicknamed "Blackbird" which may hint at its colour and imply that the others were painted differently. The docks lines at Falmouth were converted to narrow gauge in May 1892, as were the locomotives which continued to operate until 1926.

Construction of **Table Bay** Harbour, Cape Town, South Africa commenced in June 1860, using direct labour employed by the Harbour Board. Initially horses were used, but locomotives were employed from December 1862 (C98). As well as the breakwater, all the track at the harbour and the line from the harbour to the town were broad gauge until 1873, when the harbour lines were reduced to 3ft. 6in. and connected to the Cape Government Railway. The breakwater lines remained broad gauge until 1904, when they were replaced by a 2ft. gauge tramway. It appears that six broad gauge four-wheeled tank locomotives were used and that three were converted to 3ft. 6in. gauge around 1904.

Work on the artificial harbour at **Ponta Delgada**, on the island of Sao Miguel, Azores commenced on 30 September 1861, using direct labour. There was a strong Holyhead connection however, and a certain amount of equipment was purchased from the Holyhead contractors J. & C. Rigby. From January 1888 the French company Combemale et Michelon were contracted for further works. After severe storm damage in December 1894 work was suspended, later re-commenced using direct labour. The harbour continued to be improved, with further works taking place in 1937 and 1963. The railway was extended for construction of the Esplanade between 1948 and 1954. The first four-wheeled tank locomotives were delivered in 1862, eventually totalling six (C97). Three locomotives were still operational in 1961. One was later disposed of but two remain in covered storage at the port; hopefully one day they will be restored to working order. The surviving locomotives last ran in black livery with red wheels, although hardly a scrap of paint remains on them now.

The **Port Erin** Harbour of Refuge on the Isle of Man was commenced in October 1864, the Isle of Man Harbour Commissioners using direct labour. It was completed in 1876, but further work followed storm damage in 1881-82. It was totally destroyed by exceptionally heavy gales in 1884. Three steam cranes were employed, as well as one locomotive obtained second hand from the Portland Harbour contractor (C90). The locomotive was sold about 1874-75.

Construction of **East London** Harbour, South Africa commenced in 1872 using convict labour and ox carts employed by the Harbour Board. This was South Africa's only river port. Railway operation commenced in 1873, with four 0-4-0 vertical-boiler tank locomotives (C99) being delivered between then and 1879. In 1907 connection was made with the 3ft. 6in. gauge East London & Queenstown Railway on the opposite bank of the river, after which the harbour lines were altered to suit and the broad gauge locomotives disposed of.

Construction of the artificial harbour at **Horta**, on the island of Fayal, Azores commenced on 20 March 1876. Further tenders were invited in September 1887. The local museum staff believe that the railway ceased operations in 1901. Four 0-4-0ST locomotives (C96) were delivered to the railway between 1876 and 1890, all disposed of after the 1901 closure.

C11	**Vale of Neath Railway**	4-4-0ST

TOTAL: 6   PERIOD: 1851-72
BUILDER: R Stephenson & Co
CYLINDERS: 17in x 24in
DRIVING WHEELS: 5ft 6in
CARRYING WHEELS: 3ft 6in

NO.	NEW	WDN
1	10/51	12/72
2	11/51	2/72
3	11/51	6/72
4	11/51	2/72
5	12/51	12/72
6	12/51	3/72

C12	**Vale of Neath Railway**	0-6-0ST

TOTAL: 3   PERIOD: 1854-58
BUILDER: R Stephenson & Co
CYLINDERS: 17½in x 24
DRIVING WHEELS: 5ft 0in
CARRYING WHEELS: 3ft 6in

NO.	NEW	WDN
7	6/54	® 1858
8	8/54	® 1858
9	10/54	® 1858

® *Rebuilt to 0-6-0ST, see C15.*

C13   Vale of Neath Railway   0-6-0ST

TOTAL: 3   PERIOD: 1854-84
BUILDER: Vulcan Foundry
CYLINDERS: 17in x 24in
DRIVING WHEELS: 4ft 9in

NO.	NEW	WDN
10	9/54	2/80
11	10/54	2/78
12	10/54	12/84

C15   Vale of Neath Railway   0-6-0ST

TOTAL: 3   PERIOD: 1858-80
BUILDER: Rebuilt from 4-4-0ST, see C12
CYLINDERS: 17½in x 24
DRIVING WHEELS: 5ft 0in

NO.	NEW	WDN
7	® 1858	7/74
8	® 1858	2/80
9	® 1858	6/78

C14   Vale of Neath Railway   0-6-0ST

TOTAL: 3   PERIOD: 1856-60
BUILDER: Vulcan Foundry
CYLINDERS: 18in x 24in
DRIVING WHEELS: 4ft 9in

NO.	NEW	WDN
13	12/56	® 1860
14	12/56	® 1860
15	1/57	® 1860

® *Rebuilt to 0-6-0, see C17.*

C16   Vale of Neath Railway   0-6-0ST

TOTAL: 4   PERIOD: 1861-86
BUILDER: Slaughter, Grüning & Co
CYLINDERS: 17½in x 24in
DRIVING WHEELS: 4ft 6in

NO.	NEW	WDN
16	11/61	8/86
17	11/61	6/85
18	12/61	5/72
19	12/61	4/75

C17   Vale of Neath Railway   0-6-0

TOTAL: 3   PERIOD: 1860-75
BUILDER: Rebuilt from 0-6-0ST, see C14
CYLINDERS: 18in x 24in
DRIVING WHEELS: 4ft 9in

NO.	NEW	WDN
13	Ⓡ 1860	12/75 ①
14	Ⓡ 1860	6/72 ②
15	Ⓡ 1860	6/74 ②

①   13's tender had 4ft wheels
②   14 and 15s' tenders had 3ft 3in wheels.

C21   Carmarthen & Cardigan   4-4-0T

TOTAL: 2   PERIOD: 1861-72
BUILDER: Sharp, Stewart & Co
CYLINDERS: 17in x 24in
DRIVING WHEELS: 5ft 2in
CARRYING WHEELS: 3ft 3in

NAME	NEW	TO SDR	WDN
Heron	1861	9/72	Ⓡ 1872 ①
Magpie	1861	9/72	Ⓡ 1872 ①

①   Both locomotives were returned to Sharp, Stewart & Co who eventually sold them to the South Devon Railway and the Cornwall Railway respectively where they were converted to 4-4-0STs, see D46.

Above - Sharp, Stewart & Company 1247 was a 4-4-0T (C21) built in 1861 and put to work on the Carmarthen & Cardigan Railway with the name Heron. In 1872 it was sold to the South Devon Railway and moved to Newton where it was rebuilt as a 4-4-0ST.

Opposite - Vale of Neath Railway 19 was a Slaughter, Grüning & Company 0-6-0ST (C16). Built in 1861, it was the last broad gauge locomotive built for the company and ran for less than 14 years. It was photographed shunting coal trucks at Swansea with mixed gauge buffers and sliding coupling that allowed it to work with both broad and narrow rolling stock.

*The Carmarthen & Cardigan Railway had two 4-4-0STs **(C22)**. Despite being built in 1864, Etna had only a 700 gallon saddle tank, whereas those being delivered to the South Devon by that time had 1,100 gallon capacity.*

C22	Carmarthen & Cardigan	4-4-0ST

TOTAL: 2   PERIOD: 1864-92
BUILDER: Rothwell & Co
CYLINDERS: 17in x 24in
DRIVING WHEELS: 5ft 3in, later 5ft 6in
CARRYING WHEELS: 3ft 6in

NAME	GWR	NEW	TO SDR	WDN	
Etna	**2132**	1864	6/69	5/92	①
Hecla	**2133**	6/64	12/72	5/92	②

① Etna was sold to the South Devon Railway then absorbed by the GWR in 1876 when it was given a number in addition to its name, but the name was lost when it was rebuilt again at some time with a B&ER-style tank

② Hecla was sold to the South Devon Railway where it was rebuilt with an Avonside boiler and tank in 1875. It was absorbed by the GWR in 1876 when it was given a number in addition to its name.

C24	South Wales Mineral Railway

TOTAL: 5   PERIOD: 1863-81
BUILDER: Manning, Wardle & Co (MW) and others

NAME	TYPE	NEW	WDN	BUILDER	
?			1872		
?			1872		
Princess	0-4-0ST	1863	1872	MW	①
Glyncorrwg	0-4-2ST	1864	1872	MW	②
?	0-4-2ST	1866	1877	MW	③

① Rebuilt as 0-4-2ST.

② Sold to Brotherhood in 1872 then by them to the Bristol & Exeter Railway 3/74. Driving wheels 4ft 0in, carrying wheels 3ft 6in, cylinders 14in x 20in.

③ Working on the Newquay & Cornwall Junction Railway from 1869, see C52.

*The two Carmarthen & Cardigan saddle tanks **(C22)** also found their way to South Devon. The Great Western Railway gave Etna a second hand saddle tank that had originally been carried by a Bristol & Exeter locomotive. It has lost its name but the GWR always referred to B&ER and SDR locomotives by just their number anyway, in this case 2132. Despite also having a more modern chimney, it still only sports a small spectacle plate.*

C25   Llynvi Valley Railway   4-4-0ST

TOTAL: 1   PERIOD: 1863-74
BUILDER: Slaughter, Grüning & Co
CYLINDERS: 16½in x 24in
DRIVING WHEELS: 5ft 6in
CARRYING WHEELS:

NAME	NEW	TO WCR	WDN
Rosa	1/63	1/68	® 1874①

①   Sold to the West Cornwall Railway in 1868 and rebuilt as an 0-6-0ST in 1874, see C26.

C26   Llynvi Valley Railway   0-6-0ST

TOTAL: 2   PERIOD: 1862-86
BUILDER: Slaughter, Grüning & Co
CYLINDERS: 16½in x 24in
DRIVING WHEELS: 4ft 6in

NAME	GWR	NEW	TO WCR	WDN
Ada	2146	2/62	2/68	11/84
Una	2147	4/62	4/68	3/86

C27   Severn & Wye Railway   0-4-0T

TOTAL: 2   PERIOD: 1868-72
BUILDER: Fletcher, Jennings (as 3ft 8in gauge)

NAME	NEW	WDN
2	© 1868	© 1872
3	© 1868	© 1872

C28   Severn & Wye Railway   0-6-0T

TOTAL: 1   PERIOD: 1868-72
BUILDER: Fletcher, Jennings (as 3ft 8in gauge)

NAME	NEW	WDN
5 Forester	© 1868	© 1872

C29   Severn & Wye Railway   0-6-0T

TOTAL: 2   PERIOD: 1868-72
BUILDER: Avonside Engine Co (AE), Fletcher, Jennings (FJ)

NAME	NEW	WDN	
Robin Hood	1868	© 1872	FJ
Friar Tuck	1870	© 1872	AE

C31   Bristol & Gloucester   2-2-0T

TOTAL: 6   PERIOD: 1844-77
BUILDER: Stothert & Slaughter using parts from Bury, Curtis & Kennedy
CYLINDERS: 15in x 21in
DRIVING WHEELS: 6ft 6in
CARRYING WHEELS: 3ft 6in

NAME	MR Nos.	NEW	TO NDR		WDN
4 Bristol	260 360 460	6/44	6/55	**Exe**	7/70
5 Gloucester	261 361 461	7/44	11/55	**Tite**	7/70
6 Berkeley	262 362 462	7/44	5/56	**Barum**	7/70
7 Wickwar	263 363	7/44			1/53
8 Cheltenham	264 364 464	7/44	8/56	**Star**	4/77
9 Stroud	265 365 465	12/44	11/55	**Mole**	7/70

C32   Bristol & Gloucester   2-4-0

TOTAL: 3   PERIOD: 1844-70
BUILDER: Stothert & Slaughter using parts from Bury, Curtis & Kennedy
CYLINDERS: 15in x 18in
DRIVING WHEELS: 5ft 0in
CARRYING WHEELS:

NAME	MR Nos.	NEW	TO NDR		WDN	
1 Tugwell	268 368 468	9/44			9/52	
2 Industry	269 369 469	9/44	5/56	**Venus**	8/70	①
3 Pilot	270	9/44			9/51	

① *Venus was reportedly used by Thomas Brassey in 1867 for engineering contracts on the Devon & Somerset Railway, see C83.*

C33   Bristol & Gloucester   0-6-0T

TOTAL: 2   PERIOD: 1844-67
BUILDER: Stothert & Slaughter using parts from Vulcan Foundry
CYLINDERS: 16in x 21in
DRIVING WHEELS: 5ft 0in

NAME	MR Nos.	NEW	TO NDR		WDN	
10 Dreadnought	266 366 466	1842	10/57	**Dreadnought**	6/63	①
11 Defiance	267 367 467	1842	4/56	**Defiance**	10/67	②

①   *Dreadnought was sold to Robert Sharpe 6/63 for building the Truro to Falmouth line, see C93.*
②   *Defiance was sold to Thomas Brassey for engineering contracts on the Devon & Somerset Railway, see C85.*

C34   North Devon Railway   2-2-2

BUILDER: Canada Works
CYLINDERS: 15¼in x 20in
DRIVING WHEELS: 6ft 0in
CARRYING WHEELS: 3ft 6in

NAME	NEW	WDN
Dart	8/55	® 11/67
Yeo	12/57	1868

® *Dart was rebuilt to a 2-4-0, see C36.*

C35   North Devon Railway   2-2-2

TOTAL: 1   PERIOD: 1855-c.62
BUILDER: Robert Stephenson
CYLINDERS: 14in x 18in
DRIVING WHEELS: 5ft 6in
CARRYING WHEELS: 4ft 0in

NAME	NEW	WDN
Taw	© 8/55	before 1863

A 'Crewe Type' 2-4-0 built at the Canada Works in Birkenhead (C36), Creedy was used by Brassey & Ogilvie for their contract to operate the North Devon Railway. It was photographed posed on the turntable at Barnstaple. In 1863 it was transferred to the London & South Western Railway for whom it continued to operate until 1877.

C36   North Devon Railway   2-4-0

TOTAL: 1   PERIOD: 1855-77
BUILDER: Canada Works
CYLINDERS: 15¼in x 20in
DRIVING WHEELS: 5ft 0in
CARRYING WHEELS: 3ft 0in

NAME	NEW	WDN
Creedy	6/55	4/77
Dart	® 1868	4/77

® *Dart was rebuilt from a 2-2-2, see C34. The dimensions may not be those stated above for Creedy.*

C37   Midland Railway   2-2-2

TOTAL: 4   PERIOD: 1848-54
BUILDER: Sharp Brothers
CYLINDERS: 16in x 20in
DRIVING WHEELS: 6ft 6in
CARRYING WHEELS: ?

NO.	RENUMBERED	NEW	WDN
66	266 366 466	11/48	© 5/54
67	267 367 467	12/48	© 5/54
68	268 368 468	2/49	© 5/54
69	269 369 469	3/49	© 5/54

C38   Midland Railway   0-6-0

TOTAL: 2   PERIOD: 1852-54
BUILDER: Kitson & Co
CYLINDERS: 16in x 24 in
DRIVING WHEELS: 5ft 0in

NO.	RENUMBERING	NEW	WDN
290	390 490	6/52	© 5/54
291	391 491	7/52	© 5/54

C51   Torbay & Brixham Railway

TOTAL: 2   PERIOD: 1868-82
BUILDER: Avonside Engine Co (AE), E B Wilson & Co (EBW)

NAME	TYPE	NEW	WDN	BUILDER
Queen	0-4-0WT	1868	12/82	EBW①
King	2-4-0T	–	–	AE ②
Raven	0-4-0ST	1877	12/82	AE ③

① *Previously workd at Portland, see C93.*
② *Ordered by the T&BR but delivered instead to the South Devon Railway in 1871, see D47.*
③ *Purchased from Great Western Railway. It returned to their stock in 1883 and continued to work until 5/92 after which it was converted to narrow gauge. see D52.*

C52   Newquay & Cornwall Junction

TOTAL: 4?   PERIOD: 1869-77
BUILDER: Manning, Wardle & Co (MW), Brotherhood (Bh) and others

NAME	TYPE	NEW	WDN	BUILDER	
Cornwall	0-6-0T	?	?	?	①
Newquay	0-4-2ST	1869	1877	MW	②
Phoenix	?	1868?	1877	Bh?	③
Roebuck	0-6-0T	1873?	?	?	①

① *Gauge uncertain.*
② *Previously worked on South Wales Mineral Railway, see C24.*
③ *Cylinders 12in x 22in; 0-4-2T or 2-4-0T.*

C53   Lostwithiel & Fowey Railway

TOTAL: 2?   PERIOD: 1870-79

NAME	TYPE	NEW	WDN
?	?	1870	1870?
?	?	1870?	1879?

C61   Metropolitan Railway

TOTAL: 1   PERIOD: 1861
BUILDER: R Stephenson & Co
DRIVING WHEELS: 6ft 0in
CARRYING WHEELS: 4ft 0in

NAME	NEW	WDN
(Fowler's Ghost)	1861	1861

C81   Contractors locomotives

TOTAL: 3?   PERIOD: c.1837

NAME	TYPE	NEW	WDN	
Vesta		1837	?	①
Try Again		c.1837	?	①
Brothers		c.1837	?	①

① *Used by contractors during the construction of the Great Western Railway*

C83   Contractors locomotives

TOTAL: 2?   PERIOD: 1844-67
BUILDER: Vulcan Foundry (VF), Stothert & Slaughter (SS)

NAME	TYPE	NEW	WDN	BUILDER	
?	2-4-0	1844	1848	VF	①
Venus	0-4-2	1867	1867	SS	②

① *Unknown contractor for South Devon Railway construction (gauge unconfirmed).*
② *Thomas Brassey for construction of Devon & Somerset Railway. It had previously worked the North Devon Railway, see C32.*

C84   Contractors' locomotives   0-4-0T

TOTAL: 4?   PERIOD: 1856-61
BUILDER: ①Rebuilt by Bristol & Exeter Railway, see B21;
② Avonside Engine Co

NAME	TYPE	NEW	WDN	
? (Fairfield)	0-4-0vb	® 6/56	?	①
Torbay	0-4-0vb	c.1859	c.1861	③
Goat	0-4-0WT	11/90	1893	②
Owl	0-4-0WT	11/90	1893	②

① *Used by Hutchinson & Ritson in Somerset and possibly elsewhere, rebuilt from the B&ER steam carriage, see B21.*
② *Used by Pearson & Son at Ivybridge 1890-93. They were purchased from the GWR and sold back to them at the end of the contract for conversion to narrow gauge, see D51.*
③ *Possibly for Smith & Knight's Torbay & Dartmouth Railway contract. Sold for further use at Falmouth Docks, see C91.*

C85   Contractors' locomotives   0-6-0

TOTAL: 2?   PERIOD: 1842-63
BUILDER: Stothert & Slaughter using parts from Vulcan Foundry
CYLINDERS: 16in x 21in
DRIVING WHEELS: 5ft 0in

NAME	NEW	WDN	
Defiance	6/63	1863	①
Dreadnought	6/63	8/63	②

① *Defiance was used by Thomas Brassey from 6/63 for engineering contracts on the Devon & Somerset Railway. It had previously worked the North Devon Railway, see C33.*
② *Dreadnought was purchased by Robert Sharpe 6/63 for building the Truro to Falmouth line but he was unable to find another buyer for it at the end of this contract. It had previously worked the North Devon Railway, see C33.*

C86   Contractors' locomotives   0-6-0T

TOTAL: 1?   PERIOD: 1874

NAME	NEW	WDN	
?	?	1874	①

① *Used by Furniss & Buxton for Minehead Railway construction (gauge unconfirmed)*

C90   Port Erin Breakwater   0-4-0WT

TOTAL: 7?   PERIOD: c.1864-75
BUILDER: E B Wilson & Co
CYLINDERS: 10½in x 17in?
DRIVING WHEELS: 4ft 0in?

NAME	NEW	WDN	
Henry B Lock	c.1864	1875	①

① *Previously worked at Portland Breakwater.*

C91   Falmouth Docks   0-4-0vb

TOTAL: 3   PERIOD: 1861-92
BUILDER: Sara & Co
CYLINDERS: 7in x 12in

NO.	NEW	WDN	
1 (Blackbird)	c.1861	© 5/92	
2 Torbay	c.1861	© 5/92	①
3 (Billie)	c.1861	© 5/92	

① *Second-hand from a contractor, possibly Smith & Knight, see C84.*

C92   Holyhead Breakwater

TOTAL: 10?   PERIOD: c.1849-1913
BUILDER: ① R B Longridge & Co, ⑤ Neilson & Co
CYLINDERS: j 10¼in x 18in, ⑤ 12in x 18in
DRIVING WHEELS: ① 3ft 2in, ⑤ 4ft 0in

NAME	TYPE	NEW	WDN	
?	?	c.1849	?	
?	?	c.1849	?	
Prince Albert	0-4-0WT	1852	1913	①
London	0-4-0WT	c.1852	12/72	①②
Holyhead	0-4-0WT	c.1852	12/72	①②
Cambria	0-4-0WT	c.1852	12/72	①②
?	0-4-0WT	c.1852	12/72	①②③
?	0-4-0WT	?	c.1872	①④
?	0-4-0T	1/62	?	⑤
?	0-4-0T	1863	?	⑤

①   *Built by R B Longridge & Co. Wheels 3ft 2in, cylinders 10¼in x 18in.*
②   *Sold to I W Boulton, a dealer.*
③   *Possibly named* **Queen**.
④   *Possibly sold for further use at Ponta Delgada, see C97.*
⑤   *Built by Neilson & Co. Wheels 4ft 0in, cylinders 12in x 18in.*

*Queen was an 0-4-0WT built by EB Wilson for the Portland Harbour works **(C93)**, where was photographed before it was sold to the Torbay & Brixham Railway in 1868. On 1 January 1883 it became Great Western property but was withdrawn on the same day without being allocated a GWR number.*

C93   Portland Breakwater   0-4-0WT

TOTAL: 7?   PERIOD: 1851-75
BUILDER: E B Wilson & Co
CYLINDERS: l 10½in x 17in
DRIVING WHEELS: l 4ft 0in

NAME	NEW	WDN	
?	c.1851	1875	①②
Queen	1852	1868	③
?	1853	c.1864	②④⑤
Prince Albert	c.1854	1875	②⑤
Prince Alfred	c.1854	1875	②⑤
?	c.1854	1875	②⑤
?	?	1875	②⑤

①   Wheel arrangement and builder of the first locomotive is unrecorded.
②   The exact identities of Prince Albert and Prince Alfred are uncertain and the so dates ascribed to these locomotives may actually belong to one of the locomotives marked ?, and vice versa.
③   Later working on the Torbay & Brixham Railway, see C51.
④   Sold for work on Port Erin Breakwater, see C90.
⑤   Sold to I W Boulton, a dealer.

C96   Horta Harbour   0-4-0ST

TOTAL: 4   PERIOD: 1876-1901
BUILDER: Vulcan Foundry (VF), Black, Hawthorn & Co (BH)

NO.	BUILDER	NEW	WDN	
?	VF	1876	1901?	①
?	VF	1876	1901?	①
?	VF	1879	1901?	②
?	BH	1890	1901?	③

①   Cylinders 12in x 18in, driving wheels 3ft 6in.
②   Assumed to have cylinders 12in x 18in and, driving wheels 3ft 6in.
③   Cylinders 12in x 19in, driving wheels 4ft 0in.

C97   Ponta del Garda Harbour

TOTAL: 6   PERIOD: c.1872-present day
BUILDER: R B Longridge & Co (RBL), Neilson & Co (N),
       Black, Hawthorn & Co (BH), Falcon Engine Works (F)

NO.	TYPE	BUILDER	NEW	WDN	
1	0-4-0ST	N	1862	1961-66	
2	0-4-0ST	BH	1883	–	①②
3	0-4-0ST	F	1888	–	②
?	0-4-0ST	N	1863	by 1900?	
?	0-4-0T	?	?	?	
?	0-4-0WT	?	?	?	③

①   Cylinders 12in x 19in, driving wheels 4ft 0in.
②   Currently stored unserviceable.
③   Possibly previously worked at Holyhead Breakwater in which case it was built by R B Longridge & Co, see C92.

C98   Table Bay Harbour

TOTAL: 6   PERIOD: 1862-1904
BUILDER: Black, Hawthorn & Co (BH), Fletcher, Jennings & Co (FJ), Henry Hughes (HH)

NO.	TYPE	BUILDER	NEW	WDN	
?	0-4-0ST	HH?	1862	?	
?	0-4-0T?	FJ	1874	?	①
?	0-4-0WT	FJ	1879	?	①
4	0-4-0ST	BH	1881	© c.1904	②
5	0-4-0ST	BH	1881	© c.1904	②
8	0-4-0ST	BH	1893	©	②

①   Wheels 2ft 9in, cylinders 9in x 16in.
②   Wheels 2ft 10in, cylinders 11in x 17in.

C90   East London Harbour   0-4-0vb

TOTAL: 4   PERIOD: 1873-1907
BUILDER: Alexander Chaplin & Co

NO.	NEW	WDN
1?	1873	1907?
2?	1874	1907?
3?	1879	1907?
4	1879	1907?

Part D - SOUTH DEVON and CORNWALL

The South Devon Railway from Exeter to Plymouth and Torquay was designed to be worked by atmospheric traction. Engine houses were built at intervals alongside the line and stationary steam engines exhausted the air from a pipe laid between the rails. The trains had a 'piston carriage' at the head instead of a locomotive, the piston of which was suspended in the pipe and connected to the carriage through a slot in the top of the pipe that was sealed by a leather valve. These trains started running as far as Teignmouth on 13 September 1847, were extended to Newton the following January, but were abandoned on 10 September, 1848.

The first section of the SDR had opened on 30 May 1846, before the atmospheric equipment was ready. The Great Western Railway came to its aid before, during and after the atmospheric period by providing locomotives of various classes. These were mainly Leo 2-4-0s (A31) but also included 2-2-2s (A13 & A14), and 0-6-0s (A61). The two Haigh Foundry 2-2-2s (A11) were also sent down, renamed *Exe* and *Teign* for the duration of their stay. In 1849 Daniel Gooch built two novel 4-4-0STs specifically for the line, *Corsair* and *Brigand* (A42). With a swivelling bogie and the weight of their coal and water on their driving wheels, these saddle tanks were ideal for the steep and curving line west of Newton. The GWR charged 16d per train mile for providing the motive power.

At this time the SDR started to look for a new, more permanent, contract. On Brunel's advice this was not an ordinary operational contract, but rather one that allowed the company to purchase the locomotives at its end. This was eventually signed on 3 June 1851 with Edward Evans and Charles Geech, although the first locomotives were not ready until October. The charge was on a scale starting at 15d per mile for the lightest trains.

On 28 February 1859 the Cornwall Railway signed a similar contract with Edward Evans, Daniel Gooch, and Thomas Walker (who had replaced Geech as a partner) to operate their line from Plymouth to Truro which opened on 4 May that year. This contract had charges starting at 14d per mile. There is no evidence that Evans' locomotives on the SDR and CR contracts were worked on the other railway in normal operation. The SDR contract had been meant to last for ten years but with the need to provide extra locomotives for new branch lines opening in 1859, and with the Cornwall Railway having agreed their contract, the opportunity was taken to negotiate a new contract which ran from 1 July 1859 for seven years.

With both the contracts due for renewal in 1866, and the West Cornwall Railway to Penzance being converted to broad gauge, it was decided that the South Devon would buy out the contracts. Although each locomotive was still charged to one of the three railways, they were now operated as a single fleet with the running costs shared between the three railways. In the following lists, locomotives charged to the three companies are identified as:

C   Cornwall Railway
D   South Devon Railway
W West Cornwall Railway

The SDR was amalgamated into the GWR on 1 February 1876 but there was still a need to account for the Cornwall Railway separately while it remained an independent concern. From December 1884 the GWR charged six additional locomotives to the Cornwall Railway to make up for withdrawals since 1876. These were two ex-SDR passenger locomotives (D44) and four GWR goods locomotives (A64).

The first Locomotive Superintendent was William Gooch, the locomotive designer's younger brother; he was replaced in 1864 by John Wright. The main locomotive works were at Newton and repairs were also undertaken at Plymouth. The Cornwall Railway had use of this facility and also a smaller one at Truro which was moved to Falmouth when the line was extended in 1863. The West Cornwall had workshops at Carn Brea. There were also locomotive sheds at Exeter, Penzance, and on most of the branch lines. The livery was generally similar to that used by the GWR.

The first twelve 4-4-0STs designed by Daniel Gooch (D41) were delivered from October 1851 through to April 1853. Two 0-6-0STs (D61) followed in 1854 that were better suited to the heavy goods trains then running, and were identical to some under construction at the time for the Vale of Neath Railway (C13). These two basic types continued to be developed throughout the railways' independent existence, with those supplied under the 1859 contracts (D42, D62) being broadly similar except that the water capacity was increased. The first locomotives had an 800 gallon capacity, but this increased to 1,000 gallons on locomotives delivered in 1855, and 1,100 gallons from 1859. Locomotives built from 1866 (D43, D63) had conventional plate frames, unlike the earlier locomotives.

Between 1868 and 1872 a number of locomotives were bought into the fleet from other railways:

LVR	**Rosa**	W	1/68	Antelope class (C25)	①
LVR	**Ada**	W	2/68	Ada class (C26)	
LVR	**Una**	W	4/68	Ada class (C26)	
C&CR	**Etna**	D	6/69	Hecla class (C22)	
WCR	**Redruth**	W	12/71	(D66)	
WCR	**Penwith**	W	1/72	(D49)	
GWR	**Saunders**	D	2/72	Fowler class (A62)	
GWR	**Fowler**	C	6/72	Fowler class (A62)	
GWR	**Bukeley**	C	8/72	Fowler class (A62)	
GWR	**Stromboli**	D	9/72	Tornado class (A61)	
C&CR	**Heron**	D	9/72	Heron class (D46)	
C&CR	**Magpie**	C	9/72	Heron class (D46)	
C&CR	**Hecla**	D	12/72	Hecla class (C22)	

Key: *C&CR*   *Carmarthen & Cardigan Railway*
         GWR   *Great Western Railway*
         LVR   *Llynvi Valley Railway*
         WCR   *West Cornwall Railway*
         ① *Rosa was rebuilt as an Ada class (D62) in 1874.*

Several small 0-4-0 shunting locomotives were also built, mainly for working the dock lines around Plymouth. The first, *Tiny* (D50), was put to work in 1868 after the directors had seen similar vertical boiler locomotives working in the docks at Falmouth (C91). In 1873 some diminutive well tanks (D51) were delivered, but more conventional saddle tanks followed in 1874 (D52). There were also a handful of small 2-4-0 (D47, D48) and 0-6-0 (D64) tanks for the smaller branch lines.

New 4-4-0STs and 0-6-0STs were delivered from 1872, all designed as convertibles. The Stag class passenger locomotives (D44) were cut up in 1893 without ever running on the narrow gauge, but most of the Camel class 0-6-0STs (D65) were converted and ran for several more years. In all, 22 locomotives were converted by the GWR. By 1910 most except the Prince class had been sold or were used only as stationary boilers. *Prince* itself was used for many years as a stationary boiler and only cut up in 1935, while the last of three similar locomotives completed at Swindon in 1878 was operated until 1936. *Rook* was probably the last working SDR 0-4-0ST when it was withdrawn in 1929, and *Achilles* the last 0-6-0ST in 1932. Both of these had been sold out of GWR service but later returned.

	SDR	BG	CONV.	NG	
D47	**King**	2171	3/78	**2**	①
D48	**Saturn**		12/78	**1298**	
D48	**Jupiter**		12/78	**1299**	②
D48	**Mercury**		12/78	**1300**	

D48	**Prince**	2137	6/93	**1316**	
D65	**Emperor**	2167	8/93	**1317**	③
D65	**Python**	2168	5/93	**1318**	
D65	**Vulcan**	2169	4/93	**1319**	
D65	**Buffalo**	2160	10/93	**1320**	
D65	**Elephant**	2161	12/93	**1321**	
D65	**Camel**	2162	11/93	**1322**	
D65	**Dragon**	2164	6/93	**1323**	
D65	**Achilles**	2165	9/93	**1324**	③
D65	**Dromedary**	2166	5/92	**1325**	
D64	**Taurus**	2170	5/94	**1326**	
D51	**Owl**	2172	8/93	**1327**	④
D51	**Goat**	2174	8/93	**1328**	④
D52	**Raven**	2175	6/92	**1329**	⑤
D52	**Rook**	2176	3/92	**1330**	⑥
D52	**Crow**	2177	11/92	**1331**	⑥
D52	**Lark**	2178	9/92	**1332**	⑥
D52	**Jay**	2179	5/92	**1333**	⑥

① *Sold into industrial use, possibly named* **Perseverance**.
② *1298 was rebuilt and fitted out as a crane tank in 1881.*
③ *Sold to become South Wales Mineral Railway* **6** *&* **7**, *later returned to GWR as* **817** *&* **818**.
④ *Owl and Goat were fitted out as 0-4-0STs on conversion to narrow gauge.*
⑤ *Sold to the Wantage Tramway.*
⑥ *Sold to become Powesland & Mason* **7-10**. *One, believed to be Rook, returned to the GWR as* **925**.

The first 12 locomotives for the SDR were all 4-4-0STs **(D41)** *built to the same specification as the GWR's Bogie class, with 5ft 9in wheels, 17in cylinders, and an 800 gallon saddle tank that was fitted around the driving wheels. Despite being classified in later years as passenger locomotives, they handled goods trains too until 1854 when the first 0-6-0STs were built. Falcon was built by the Haigh Foundry in 1852. By the time this photograph was taken the footplate, which originally only covered the driving wheels, had been extended and the spectacle plate had also been raised to provide a little more protection to the crew.*

D41   Comet class   4-4-0ST

TOTAL: 12   PERIOD: 1851-84
BUILDER: See below: William Fairburn & Sons (Fb), Haigh Foundry (HF), R B Longridge & Co (RBL), Stothert & Slaughter (SS)
CYLINDERS: 17in x 24in
DRIVING WHEELS: 5ft 9in
CARRYING WHEELS: 3ft 6in

NAME	GWR	NEW	WDN		
Comet	2096	10/51	6/84	D	RBL
Lance		10/51	12/73	D	RBL
Rocket	2097	10/51	10/77	D	RBL
Meteor	2098	11/51	7/81	D	RBL
Priam	2100	11/51	11/76	D	HF
Aurora	2099	1/52	11/78	D	RBL
Damon	2101	2/52	3/76	D	HF
Ostrich	2104	8/52	12/77	D	Fb
Falcon	2102	9/52	11/78	D	HF
Orion	2103	2/53	4/78	D	HF
Ixion	2105	4/53	3/78	D	SS
Osiris		4/53	8/73	D	SS

D42   Antelope class   4-4-0ST

TOTAL: 16   PERIOD: 1859-92
BUILDER: Slaughter, Grüning & Co
CYLINDERS: 16½in x 24in
DRIVING WHEELS: 5ft 6in
CARRYING WHEELS: 3ft 6in

NAME	GWR	NEW	WDN		
Hawk	2108	4/59	12/85	C	
Eagle	2106	4/59	9/76	C	
Elk	2107	4/59	3/77	C	
Lynx	2109	4/59	12/76	C	
Gazelle	2110	5/59	6/85	C	
Mazeppa	2111	5/59	6/85	C	
Giraffe	2112	6/59	10/77	D	
Lion	2113	6/59	12/83	D	
Antelope	2114	7/59	11/84	C	
Wolf	2115	8/59	6/78	C	
Tiger	2116	5/60	12/84	D	
Hector	2117	8/60	1/92	D	
Cato	2118	9/63	10/77	C	
Dart	2119	12/64	6/85	D	
Pollux	2120	5/65	12/82	C	①
Castor	2121	6/65	9/82	C	①

① *Pollux and Castor were ordered as* **Tamar** *and* **Fal**.

*The contracts let in 1859 saw the delivery of slightly smaller bogie tanks (**D42**) with 5ft 6in wheels and 16½ in cylinders, but the more conventional saddle tanks now extended back over the firebox and so carried 1,100 gallons. Seen here in original condition, Hawk was delivered to the Cornwall Railway in May 1859 for the opening of the line from Plymouth to Truro. When it was withdrawn in 1885 it had run 837,571 miles – the greatest mileage of any broad gauge locomotive without a boiler change.*

Above - In 1866 some new 4-4-0STs were delivered for the West Cornwall and Launceston services, including Zebra seen here in final condition with a cab and running as GWR 2127. This batch (D43) reverted to 17in cylinders powering 5ft 8in wheels but with the same 1,100 gallon tanks used since 1859.

Four 5ft 9in 4-4-0STs were built by the Avonside Engine Company in the 1870s to two slightly different designs. Osiris was built to the second design **(D44)** *in 1875, the last locomotive to be delivered to the SDR although in 1884 it was transferred to the Cornwall Railway fleet. All four were designed as convertibles and were kept at Swindon for a while after the end of broad gauge services but were condemned in March 1893 without being converted to narrow gauge.*

D43   Zebra class   4-4-0ST

TOTAL: 6   PERIOD: 1866-92
BUILDER: Avonside Engine Co
CYLINDERS: 17in x 24in
DRIVING WHEELS: 5ft 8in
CARRYING WHEELS: 3ft 4in

NAME	GWR	NEW	WDN	
Sedley	2124	9/66	12/85	D
Gorgon	2122	9/66	5/92	W
Titan	2126	10/66	11/86	W
Pluto	2123	10/66	5/92	W
Zebra	2127	10/66	5/92	W
Sol	2125	11/66	5/92	D

D44   Stag class   4-4-0ST

TOTAL: 4   PERIOD: 1872-92
BUILDER: Avonside Engine Co
CYLINDERS: 17in x 24in
DRIVING WHEELS: 5ft 9in

CARRYING WHEELS: 3ft 6in

NAME	GWR	NEW	WDN	
Leopard	2128	12/72	5/92	D
Stag	2129	12/72	5/92	D
Lance	2130	2/75	5/92	D ①
Osiris	2131	3/75	5/92	D ①

①   *Lance and Osiris were charged to Cornwall Railway from 12/84*

D46   Heron class   4-4-0ST

TOTAL: 3   PERIOD: 1872-92
BUILDER: South Devon Railway using parts from Sharp, Stewart & Co
CYLINDERS: 17in x 24in
DRIVING WHEELS: 5ft 3in
CARRYING WHEELS: 3ft 3in

NAME	GWR	NEW	WDN	
Heron	2134	® 9/72	5/92	D
Magpie	2135	® 9/72	3/89	C

Heron and Magpie were built using parts from Sharp, Stewart & Co 4-4-0Ts previously used on the Carmarthen & Cardigan Railway, see C21.

Heron was a 4-4-0ST **(D46)** *built at Newton in 1872 using parts supplied from Sharp, Stewart & Company. It had previously run as a side tank on the Carmarthen & Cardigan Railway. Its 5ft 3in wheels and 900 gallon tank meant it was smaller than the other 4-4-0STs but it saw out the end of the broad gauge.*

*In 1871 a 2-4-0ST was built at Newton using parts supplied by the Ince Forge Company (**D48**). Prince proved a successful design for branch line work and three more were in course of erection when the railway was amalgamated with the GWR. These were completed at Swindon as narrow gauge 2-4-0Ts and found use on West Country branch lines; the GWR provided more 2-4-0STs for broad gauge branches by fitting tanks to 10 Hawthorn Class locomotives (A44) in 1877.*

D47	King		2-4-0T

TOTAL: 1   PERIOD: 1871-78
BUILDER: Avonside Engine Co
CYLINDERS: 9in x 16in
DRIVING WHEELS: 3ft 0in
CARRYING WHEELS: 2ft 6in

NAME	GWR	NEW	WDN
King	**2171**	1/71	Ⓒ 3/78 *D*

D48	Prince		2-4-0ST

TOTAL: 1   PERIOD: 1871-92
BUILDER: South Devon Railway using parts from Ince
       Forge Co
CYLINDERS: 12in x 17in (j 11½in x 17in)
DRIVING WHEELS: 4ft 0in
CARRYING WHEELS: 3ft 0in

NAME	GWR	NEW	WDN
Prince	**2137**	6/71	5/92 *D*
Saturn	–	–	*D* ①
Jupiter	–	–	*D* ①
Mercury	–	–	*D* ①

①   *Saturn, Jupiter and Mercury were under construction by the South Devon Railway at Newton when the South Devon Railway amalgamated with the Great Western Railway. They were completed at Swindon as narrow gauge 2-4-0Ts 1298 - 1300.*

D49	Penwith		2-4-0ST

TOTAL: 1   PERIOD: 1872-88
BUILDER: Stothert & Slaughter
CYLINDERS: 15in x 22in
DRIVING WHEELS: 5ft 0in
CARRYING WHEELS: 3ft 0in

NAME	GWR	NEW	WDN
Penwith	**2136**	Ⓒ 1/72	12/88 *W*

Penwith was rebuilt from a West Cornwall Railway narrow gauge 2-4-0.

D50	Tiny		0-4-0vb

TOTAL: 1   PERIOD: 1868-83
BUILDER: Sara & Co
CYLINDERS: 9in x 12in
DRIVING WHEELS: 3ft 0in

NAME	GWR	NEW	WDN
Tiny	**2180**	1/68	6/83 *D*

Tiny became a stationary engine at Newton Abbot and is now preserved.

*The only surviving broad gauge locomotive that once ran on the GWR is Tiny. Not a typical example, this vertical-boilered four-wheeler (**D50**) was bought by the SDR to replace horses working on the Sutton Harbour branch in Plymouth after the directors had seen similar locomotives working in the docks at Falmouth (C91). It is seen here after retirement to Newton Abbot Works where it was used as a stationary engine. In 1927 it was put on display at the adjacent station; it has since been moved to the railway museum at Buckfastleigh.*

D51	Weasel			0-4-0WT

TOTAL: 3   PERIOD: 1873-93
BUILDER: Avonside Engine Co
DRIVING WHEELS: 3ft 0in
CYLINDERS: 11in x 16in

NAME	GWR	NEW	WDN	SOLD	
Owl	2172	1/73	5/89	11/90 D	①
Goat	2174	2/73	12/85	11/90 D	①
Weasel	2173	3/73	12/82	–	D

① *Owl and Goat were sold to S Pearson & Son who sold them back to the Great Western Railway in 1893 and they were subsequently converted to narrow gauge 0-4-0STs.*

D52	Raven		0-4-0ST

TOTAL: 5   PERIOD: 1874-92
BUILDER: Avonside Engine Co
DRIVING WHEELS: 3ft 0in
CYLINDERS: 14in x 18in

NAME	GWR	NEW	WDN	
Raven	2175	11/74	© 5/92 D	①
Rook	2176	11/74	© 11/91 D	
Lark	2178	12/74	© 5/92 D	
Crow	2177	12/74	© 5/92 D	
Jay	2179	2/75	© 2/92 D	

① *Raven was sold to the Torbay & Brixham Railway 1/77 and returned to the Great Western Railway 1/83.*

Following Tiny, three rather more conventional shunting locomotives **(D51)** were delivered in 1873. After withdrawal Goat and Owl were sold to the contractors who were engaged on widening the line near Ivybridge. When this work was complete they were repurchased by the GWR and converted to narrow gauge. They are seen at Swindon surrounded by other convertible locomotives: 1076 class 0-6-0STs behind and ex-SDR 0-6-0ST Prince on the right.

The final batch of shunting tanks were 0-4-0STs **(D52)** such as Rook. They were fitted with mixed gauge buffers and coupling to enable them to work with either broad or narrow gauge vehicles. They were a familiar sight here at the Plymouth Great Western Docks or shunting at Newton, but sister locomotive Raven spent six years on the Torbay & Brixham Railway during which time it worked passenger trains. In 1892 they were converted to narrow gauge, Rook becoming number 1330. In 1906 it was sold to Powesland & Mason for working at Swansea Harbour. When this partnership's locomotives were sold to the GWR in 1924 number 7 became GWR 925, eventually being withdrawn in 1929.

70

D61　　　Tornado class　　　0-6-0ST

TOTAL: 4　　PERIOD: 1854-85
BUILDER: Vulcan Foundry
CYLINDERS: 17in x 24in
DRIVING WHEELS: 4ft 9in

NAME	GWR	NEW	WDN	
Volcano	2140	11/54	10/77	*D*
Tornado	2139	12/54	12/84	*D*
Sampson	2142	9/55	6/84	*D*
Goliah	2141	9/55	6/85	*D*

D62　　　Ada class　　　0-6-0ST

TOTAL: 5 ①　　PERIOD: 1860-87
BUILDER: Slaughter, Grüning & Co
CYLINDERS: 16½in x 24in
DRIVING WHEELS: 4ft 6in

NAME	GWR	NEW	WDN	
Dido	2143	3/60	10/77	*C*
Hero	2144	4/60	2/87	*C*
Rosa	2145	® 1874	10/85	*W*

® *Rosa was rebuilt from a 4-4-0ST, see C25.*

① *Class total of 5 includes two ex-Llynvi Valley Railway locomotives, see C26*

D63　　　Romulus class　　　0-6-0ST

TOTAL: 8　　PERIOD: 1860-92
BUILDER: Slaughter, Grüning & Co (①　Avonside Engine Co)
CYLINDERS: 17in x 24in
DRIVING WHEELS: 4ft 9in

NAME	GWR	NEW	WDN		
Hebe	2148	4/60	11/77	*D*	
Ajax	2149	9/60	6/84	*D*	
Brutus	2150	10/62	12/84	*D*	
Argo	2151	10/63	5/92	*C*	
Atlas	2152	10/63	10/85	*C*	
Juno	2153	12/64	6/84	*D*	
Romulus	2155	11/66	5/92	*W*	①
Remus	2154	11/66	11/86	*W*	①

① *By 1866 Slaughter, Grüning & Co had become the Avonside Engine Co.*

0-6-0ST (D63) Argo was supplied to the Cornwall Railway as an additional goods locomotive when the Falmouth extension opened in 1863. Goods locomotives went through similar development to the passenger 4-4-0STs; Argo had 16½in cylinders and a 1,100 gallon tank. The Cornwall Railway locomotives were numbered into the GWR fleet in February 1876 and it is seen with number 2151 but still without a proper cab.

*A number of small tank locomotives were purchased by the SDR for branch line working. Taurus was a unique 0-6-0ST **(D64)** from the Avonside Engine Company in Bristol with 3ft wheels and 12½in cylinders.*

D64		**Taurus**		0-6-0ST

.TOTAL: 1   PERIOD: 1869-92
BUILDER: Avonside Engine Co
CYLINDERS: 12½in x 16in
DRIVING WHEELS: 3ft 0in

NAME	GWR	NEW	WDN	
Taurus	**2170**	5/69	© 5/92	*D*

Dragon	2164	9/73	© 5/92	*C*
Achilles	2165	12/73	© 5/92	*D*
Dromedary	2166	12/73	© 4/92	*D*
Emperor	2167	12/73	© 5/92	*C*
Python	2168	3/74	© 5/92	*D*
Vulcan	2169	3/74	© 5/92	*D*

D66		**Redruth**		0-6-0ST

TOTAL: 1   PERIOD: 1871-87
BUILDER: Rebuilt
CYLINDERS: 17in x 24in
DRIVING WHEELS: 4ft 9in

NAME	GWR	NEW	WDN	
Redruth	**2156**	© 12/71	3/87	*W*

Redruth was rebuilt from a West Cornwall Railway narrow gauge 0-6-0.

D65	**Camel class**	0-6-0ST

TOTAL: 10   PERIOD: 1872-92
BUILDER: Avonside Engine Co
CYLINDERS: 17in x 24in
DRIVING WHEELS: 4ft 9in

NAME	GWR	NEW	WDN	
Buffalo	**2160**	6/72	© 5/92	*D*
Elephant	**2161**	7/72	© 5/92	*D*
Camel	**2162**	8/72	© 5/92	*D*
Hercules	**2163**	8/72	12/89	*C*

*The final batch of 0-6-0STs for the SDR group included **(D65)** Dragon. Although a Cornwall Railway locomotive it is seen here on the Launceston branch, illustrating the indiscriminate exchange of locomotives between the three railways. All but one of these ten saddle tanks were converted to narrow gauge, the last being withdrawn in 1932.*

*The South Devon also worked the West Cornwall Railway, which converted two of their narrow gauge locomotives to run on the broad gauge, although they seem to have spent most of their time working in the Plymouth area. Redruth **(D66)** was built by the WCR as an 0-6-0 tender locomotive in 1865 using parts supplied by Slaughter, Grüning & Company (which later became the Avonside Engine Company) and was converted to a broad gauge saddle tank in 1871.*

Appendix 1 - Chronological List of Types

The following table shows the years of delivery of locomotives, also significant rebuilds.

	GWR	B&ER	SDR	VoNR
1837	A11, A12			
1838	A01, A02, A11			
1839	A11, A12			
1840	A11, A12, A13, A14			
1841	A12, A13, A14, A31			
1842	A13, A14, A31, A51			
1843				
1844				
1845				
1846	A15, A25, A53			
1847	A15, A17, A53, A54			
1848	A17, A54			
1849	A17, A21, A24, A42	B11, B21, B51		
1850	A17			
1851	A17, A56	B22	D41	C11
1852	A56, A57, A61		D41	
1853	A57	B23, B51	D41	
1854	A17, A42, A57, A61	B23	D61	C12, C13
1855	A17, A32, A42, A57	B41	D61	
1856	A33, A57	B41, B53		C14
1857	A57			C14
1858	A57			C15
1859	A57	B24, B25	D42	
1860		B51	D42, D62, D63	C17
1861	A57			C16
1862	A43, A57	B25, B42	D62	
1863	A33, A43, A57		D42, D62	
1864	A33, A43		D42, D62	
1865	A34, A35, A58		D42	
1866	A35, A62, A58	B42, B61	D43, D62	
1867		B42, B61		
1868		B26	D50, C22, C25, C26	
1869				
1870	A18	B31, B52, B62		
1871	A18	B31		
1872		A58, B31, B43, B44	A61, A62, C22, D44, D46, D65	
1873	A18	A58, B26, B43	D51, D65	
1874		A58, B32, B44	D52, D65	
1875		B32	D44, D52	
1876	A18, A64			
1877	A44, B12			
1878	A18, A64			
1879				
1880	A18			
1881				
1882				
1883				
1884	A59, A64			
1885	A45			
1886	A36			
1887	A59, A64			
1888	A18, A37, A46, A59, A64			
1889	A46, A47			
1890	A38, A47			
1891	A19, A38, A47			
1892				

Appendix 2 - List of Builders

Adams, W R B21

Avonside Engine Co B43, C29, C51, C84, D43-46, D47, D51-52, D63-65

Beyer Peacock & Co B42

Black Hawthorn & Co C97, C98

Bristol & Exeter Railway B25-26, B31-32, B44, B61

Brotherhood B63, C52

Bury, Curtis & Kennedy C31, C32

Canada Works C34, C36

Chaplin, Alexander & Co C99

Falcon Engine Works C97

Fenton Murray & Jackson A13, A31

Fairburn, William & Sons D41

Fire Fly Trust A91

Fletcher Jennings C27-29, C98

Great Western Ry A15-19/33/35-37/42/43/45-47/53-59/61/62/64/91

Haigh Foundry A11, D41

Hawthorn, R & W A01-02, A14, A31, A42

Hughes, Henry C98

Ince Forge Co D48

Jones, Turner & Evans A13

Kitson & Co A43, C38

Longridge, R B & Co A13, B11, B22, C92; C97; D41

Manning Wardle & Co B45, C24, C52

Mather Dixon A11

Nasmyth Gaskell & Co A13, A51

Neilson & Co C92, C97

Rennie, G & J A13

Resco (Railways) Ltd A91

Rothwell & Co A17, A31, B23-24, B41, C22

Sara & Co C91, D50

Sharp Brothers C37

Sharp Roberts A11, A13-14

Sharp Stewart & Co C21

South Devon Railway D46, D48

Slaughter & Grüning C16, C25-26, D42, D62, D63

Stephenson, R & Co A12, A32, C11, C12, C35, C61

Stothert & Slaughter (& Co) A13/14/35/52, B11/51, C31-33, C83, C85, D41/49

Tayleur, Charles A11

Vulcan Foundry A43, B42, C13-14, C33, C83, C85, C97; D61

Wilson, E B B22, C51, C90, C93

Worcester Engine Co B52

Appendix 3 - Index of Operators

Appendix 4 - Index of Locomotives

Similarly named locomotives are separated by a semi-colon such as: A13; A35
A rebuilding or change of operator resulting in a new code is denoted by a slash such as: A35/A44
Parentheses indicate that the name was probably not carried on the locomotive such as (D42)

Bristol & Exeter Railway

1	B11; ①	29	B21; B25
2	B11; B31	30	B22; ①
3	B11; ①	31	B22
4 - 6	B11; B31	32	B22
7	B11	33	B22; ①
8	B11; B31	34	B22; B32
9 - 10	B11	35 - 38	B51
11	B11; B32	39 - 42	B23; B26
12	B11; B25	43 - 46	B23; B31
13	B11	47 - 52	B41
14	B11; B31	53	B51
15	B11	54	B51/B62
16	B11; ①	55	B51
17 - 19	B11	56	B51/B62
20	B11; B32	57 - 58	B24
21 - 28	B51	59 - 60	B51

61 - 74	B42
75 - 76	B61
77 - 82	B52
83 - 84	①
85 - 90	B43
91 - 92	B44
93 - 95	①
96 - 109	A58
110	B45
111	B63
112 - 113	②
114 - 125	①

① *4ft 8½in gauge locomotives*
② *3ft 0in gauge locomotives*

Bristol & Gloucester Railway / Midland Railway

1 - 3	C32	268 - 270	C32	460 - 462	C31
4 - 9	C31	290 - 291	C38	464 - 465	C31
10 - 11	C33	360 - 365	C31	466 - 467	C33
66 - 69	C37	366 - 367	C33	468 - 469	C32
260 - 265	C31	368 - 369	C32	490 - 491	C38
266 - 267	C33	390 - 391	C38		

Vale of Neath Railway / Great Western Railway

1 - 6	C11	2058	B45	2148 - 2153	D62
7	C12/C15	2059	B51	2154 - 2155	D63
8	C12/C15; A36	2060	B62	2156	D66
9	C12/C15	2061	B51	2157 - 2159	A62/A63
10 - 12	C13	2062	B62	2160 - 2169	D65
13	C14/C17	2063 - 2076	B51	2170	D64
14	C14/C17; A37	2077 - 2090	A58	2171	D47
15	C14/C17	2091	B63	2172 - 2174	D51
16	C16; A37	2092 - 2093	B61	2175 - 2179	D52
17 - 19	C16	2094 - 2095	B44	2180	D50
1196 - 1215	A59	2096 - 2105	D41	3021 - 3028	A19
1228 - 1257	A64	2106 - 2121	D42	3501 - 3502	A45/A38
1561 - 1580	A64	2122 - 2127	D43	3503 - 3504	A45
2001 - 2003	B26/B12	2128 - 2129	D44	3505	A45/A38
2004	B26	2130 - 2131	D45	3506	A45
2005 - 2006	B25	2132 - 2133	C22	3507 - 3508	A45/A38
2007 - 2014	B11	2134 - 2135	D46	3509 - 3510	A45
2015 - 2024	B31	2136	D49	3541 - 3542	A46/A47
2025 - 2027	B32	2137	D48	3543	A46
2028 - 2033	B41	2138	A61	3544 - 3546	A46/A47
2034 - 2047	B42	2139 - 2142	D61	3547	A46
2048 - 2053	B43	2143 - 2144	D62	3548 - 3559	A46/A47
2054 - 2055	B22	2145	C25/D62	3560	A47
2056 - 2057	B24	2146 - 2147	C26		